HOW TO BBQ EVERYTHING

HOW TO BBQ EVERYTHING

JIM MOORE

EBURY
PRESS

INTRODUCTION	6
STARTERS & SIDES	36
VEGGIE	66
PORK	88
Seafood	110
LAMB	132
CHICKEN	144
BEEF	166
SWEET	206
RUBS, SAUCES & CONDIMENTS	222
INDEX	250
THANKS	254

WELCOME TO

HOW TO BBQ EVERYTHING

Around 10 years ago, alongside two friends, I ventured into the world of 'Competition BBQ'. Camaraderie and a few cold beers spurred the team on to become two-time Irish BBQ champions. That journey was a testament to the power of community and, of course, friendly rivalry across the barricades here in Northern Ireland via the world of barbecue, drawing us together from north, west and east Belfast. What began as a desire to master the art of cooking a perfect steak transformed into an all-consuming passion, leading me to share my recipes and discoveries with you.

I've been posting my culinary escapades on social media under the handle @onlyslaggin since 2011. I've been fortunate enough to connect with over 2 million of you who share my passion for cooking over live fire. Your encouragement has inspired me to take the leap and write my first cookbook.

In Ireland, 'slagging' means affectionate teasing – a bit of good-natured banter between mates. It is an ode to friendships and humour and, to me, it embodies the joy of gathering around great food and having fun with loved ones. This ethos behind @onlyslaggin perfectly encapsulates what barbecue means to me: plenty of banter, hearty laughter and wonderful memories made over delicious meals. Cooking outdoors is an exhilarating experience that keeps me engaged, constantly adapting to the evolving nature of the flames and smoke. It's a world where set temperatures are mere suggestions, and the magic happens in the unpredictability of live fire. But don't worry, I'll share plenty of tips and tricks throughout this book to help make your barbecue journey easier and more enjoyable.

My love for cooking was ignited in my grandmother's kitchen, where I spent countless hours watching her whip up pancakes, soda bread and scones, all while sneaking samples hot off the wood-fired griddle. This early inspiration led me to work in an American-style restaurant during my teens, where I eagerly absorbed knowledge from the chefs working in the kitchen around me.

Drawing wide inspiration from my travels across the USA, Australia, Mexico, the Middle East and Europe, my recipes reflect a melting pot of influences and are aimed at being inspirational, achievable and realistic for the everyday home cook. Whether you're firing up a gas, pellet or charcoal grill – or even using your kitchen hob and oven – these recipes are designed to bring the joy of barbecue into your home. I say home, not kitchen, as barbecue, in my mind, is rustic, home-cooked food done well and enjoyed with the ones you love and want to spend time with and invite into your home.

We will start at the **basics of grill setup** to achieve success, covering the **essential accessories** as well as those that are nice to have. Following this, we will delve into some of the more technical aspects that actually make a massive difference to your finished cook: **fuel, fire lighting and management, grill selection, seasoning, resting** and **carving.** Additionally, I'll provide some quick cheat reference guides for checking temperatures and illustrations for those grill setups.

With easy-to-follow chapters, my recipes are for all levels; whether you're a beginner or intermediate or advanced in experience, I'm here to help guide you along a path to becoming a backyard hero, with chapters featuring:

STARTERS & SIDES
VEGGIE
PORK
SEAFOOD
LAMB
CHICKEN
BEEF
SWEET
RUBS, SAUCES & CONDIMENTS

I hope you feel inspired to try new techniques and flavours as you flip through this book. I invite you to dog-ear the corners of pages and write your thoughts and ideas in the margins. Let's embark on this delicious journey together – your adventure in outdoor cooking and hero status awaits!

GETTING STARTED

TOP 10 STEPS FOR GETTING BARBECUE-READY

1. **INSPECT THE GRILL** – The day before you need to use the barbecue, check for rust, wear and faulty parts like burners or hinges.

2. **CLEAN THOROUGHLY** – Especially if the barbecue has been sitting unused for a while; scrape the grates, empty ash or grease trays and clean the interior (also do this the day before).

3. **CHECK FUEL** – Make sure you have enough charcoal, gas, pellets or wood (again, do this the day before).

4. **PREHEAT WITH PURPOSE** – Light your grill early and give it time to get up to temperature. A proper preheat helps burn off any residue, sterilises the grates and ensures even cooking. This step replaces step 2 if the barbecue is in frequent use.

5. **SEASON YOUR GRATES** – After preheating, brush the hot grates and rub them with an oiled cloth or half an onion to create a non-stick surface and add subtle flavour.

6. **ORGANISE AND KNOW YOUR HEAT ZONES** – Set up your grill for the style of cook you have planned, always having a direct/indirect cooking area if possible.

7. **PREP FOOD IN ADVANCE** – Trim, marinate, season and chop ingredients before you light the grill. Let meat come to room temperature before cooking – taking the chill off your proteins for 20–30 minutes helps them cook more evenly.

8. **PAT MEAT DRY WITH KITCHEN PAPER BEFORE APPLYING RUBS OR MARINADES** – this helps to build a better crust and avoids steaming.

9. **SET UP TOOLS** – Have tongs, thermometer, trays and chopping boards ready.

10. **SEASON PROPERLY, REST THE MEAT** – Season before grilling and always rest afterwards to retain moisture and flavour.

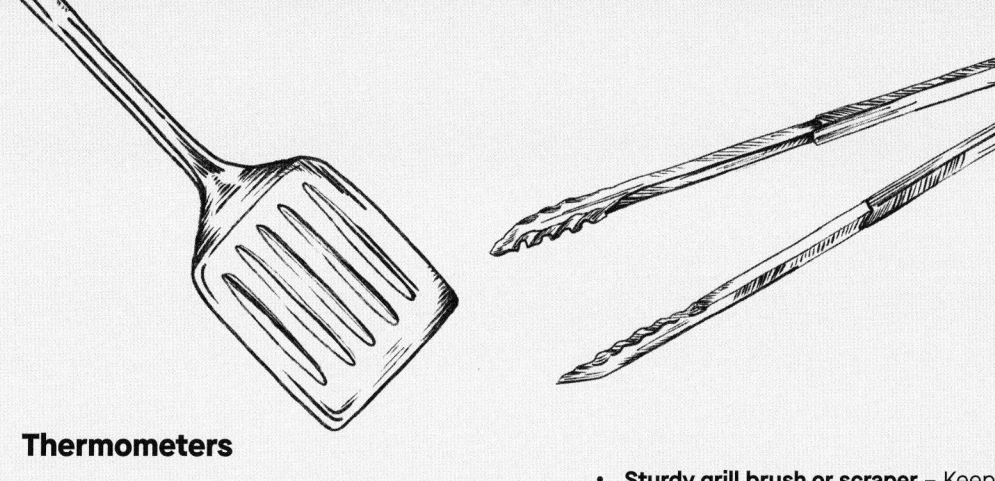

Thermometers

I can't stress this enough, but investing in a top-quality instant-read thermometer (like a Thermapen) is an absolute must-have accessory to add to your cooking arsenal. Cooking to internal temperature rather than time is the biggest game changer, helping you nail any of your meals, while reassuring you that they are safely cooked.

Aside from instant-read thermometers, there are others where you can leave the meat probe in the protein throughout the cook, which will allow you to watch its progress and monitor the food's internal temperature. These fall into the nice-to-have accessories after the instant-read thermometer.

Must-Haves

- **Long-handled tongs** – The backbone of barbecuing. Look for strong, spring-loaded tongs with a good grip and enough length to keep your hands away from the heat.

- **Instant-read thermometer** – Absolutely non-negotiable for perfect doneness. Fast, accurate temperature readings will help you avoid undercooked chicken or overcooked steak.

- **Chimney starter** – For non-kamado charcoal users, this is a game changer. Lights your coals evenly and quickly, without needing nasty lighter fluids.

- **Heat-resistant gloves** – Essential for handling hot grates, cast-iron pans or even lifting meat. Buy silicone or leather gloves – just make sure they're built for those high barbecue temperatures.

- **Sturdy grill brush or scraper** – Keeps your grates clean between cooks and helps maintain flavour and safety. Opt for bristle-free scrapers or coil-style brushes.

- **Cast-iron pan** – Adds versatility to your barbecue and is ideal for searing, frying eggs or cooking delicate sides like onions, prawns or flatbreads.

- **Spray bottle or mop brush** – Great for adding moisture and layering flavour on ribs, brisket or chicken as they cook. A mop can easily be made by tying some herbs to the handle of a wooden spoon, which will also assist in adding and building subtle flavours

Nice-to-Haves

There is a plethora of add-ons and accessories out there for barbecuing, and aside from those listed above, for me they all fall into the nice-to-have category. They aren't essential but they will allow you to push a little further on with what's possible on the barbecue.

- **Digital monitoring thermometer** (with multiple probes) – Allows you to monitor several proteins or grill zones at once – especially useful for low 'n' slow cooks.

- **Cast-iron cookware** – you may already have a good-quality cast-iron pan or Dutch oven in your kitchen. These will work well on the barbecue.

- **Additional cooking accessories** – Cedar planks, grill baskets, rib racks, fish baskets, veg grill pans, etc., any that will fall into occasional use is really a nice-to-have accessory.

SHOULD I COOK IN CELSIUS or FAHRENHEIT?

This generally depends on where you live and what you're used to.

The barbecue community traditionally prefers Fahrenheit because most US-based traditional barbecue recipes and smokers coming out of the US are calibrated in Fahrenheit. That being said, in the UK most grills show both.

I prefer working in Celsius as that's what I've grown up using and it makes sense to me. I will, however, include Fahrenheit conversions throughout.

Most thermometers, especially the ones I've mentioned earlier, will display both Celsius and Fahrenheit and allow you to switch between them easily. I would recommend that you don't jump between °C and °F, but always stick with one. That way, you don't get yourself confused.

GRILL TEMPERATURES

I will refer to grilling, roasting and smoking throughout this book. Generally, this falls into the following temperatures.

- → **GRILLING:**
  230–315°C (450–600°F), means cooking directly over the fire.

- → **ROASTING:**
  200–230°C (400–450°F), means cooking indirectly away from the primary heat source and not directly over the fire.

- → **SMOKING:**
  120–150°C (250–300°F), similar to roasting but at a lower cooking temperature over a much more extended period of time. It is often used to help break down the collagens and tough connective tissues in larger, tougher cuts of meat like brisket and pork shoulder, etc.

PLANNING YOUR COOK

All cooking requires some element of planning, but when we started as a barbecue team we didn't have a plan, so to a large extent we 'winged it' at times.

There is nothing wrong with 'winging it', but I always remember being told, 'Fail to prepare, prepare to fail...' so I like to be a lot more methodical and often I'll create a cooking plan. It's not something I do for a simple midweek meal, but particularly on longer or large cooks I find it helpful. I even do this when creating videos for Instagram, etc.

For me, it can look something like this:

PAGE 1
- List all the ingredients as a check/shopping list.
- Trim any proteins, if required.
- Wash and prep veg, etc.

PAGE 2
I fill in this prep and cook list in reverse, based on timing, so I'll start with when I want to serve/eat and work backwards.

- *18:00 – carve and serve*
- *17:00 – rest in a cooler*
- *16:00 – check temperatures and probe for tenderness*
- *15:30 – prep sides ready to go on*

And the list goes all the way back to removing the meat from the fridge, rubbing it, and even lighting and stabilising the grills.

This makes it straightforward to lay out a clear plan and guide for cooking and can be completed in less than 5 minutes, with some air of freedom and fudge factor built in. It's always much easier to have a written plan than trying to hold it all in your head and worrying you've forgotten something. For me, this removes a lot of the stress from larger cooks as I simply tick off the stages as I go. If the proteins are 'stalling' and taking longer than expected, I can add time onto the sides start time, etc. If the proteins suddenly accelerate to the finish temperatures, it's fine. I can rest them in a warm area or a cooler, and they will remain warm until I need them.

FUEL

Charcoal and wood are not just fuel sources, they are essential seasonings; they add their subtle flavours and colour to the food we cook. That is part of the enjoyment. Simple changes can transform recipes, and I encourage you to do that as you progress.

CHARCOAL

Charcoal's been around for thousands of years, used for smelting metals, heating homes and, yes, cooking meat over fire. That same method still fuels modern barbecue pits today, from the back gardens of Belfast to the brisket joints of Texas.

Charcoal isn't just a fuel, it's the foundation. Whether you're chasing the bark on a brisket or flash-searing a steak, the way you build your fire determines the success of your cook. So, take a minute to choose your charcoal, stack it with purpose, and let the flames work their magic.

There are lots of different types to choose from, so I've listed them below along with their pros, cons and what I consider them to be best used for, or when they should be avoided.

Briquettes
(Avoid using briquettes in ceramic grills, purely due to the volume of ash they produce, which could affect the airflow.)

Briquettes are the most commonly used charcoal type and are readily available at most stores and supermarkets. They aren't all created equal, so look for those marked as natural or all-natural. Briquettes are usually uniform in shape and provide a consistent, even burn, often over 1–3 hours. Their regular size and shape enable even heat distribution, making them a solid choice for beginners and various grilling methods, including low and slow barbecuing.

PROS
- Even, consistent burn.
- Long-lasting heat.
- Cheap and widely available.

CONS
- Slower to light.
- More ash production.
- Some brands contain fillers, chemicals or starch-based binders.

BEST FOR:
- Long cooks, kettle grills and offset smokers.

Lump charcoal
Lump charcoal consists of whole pieces of wood subjected to high heat to create a clean burn. As a natural product, the size may vary, which can lead to uneven heat distribution. However, lump charcoal burns hotter than briquettes, making it ideal for high-temperature grilling. The average burn time would be around 1 hour if the airflow is not constrained. It is also easier to light than briquettes.

PROS
- Burns hotter.
- Lights faster.
- Leaves less ash.
- No additives or binders.
- Reacts quickly to airflow adjustments (great for kamado and ceramic grills).

CONS
- Burns quicker.
- Irregular sizes can lead to inconsistent heat.
- Can be pricier than briquettes.

BEST FOR:
- Fast sears, open-fire grilling, ceramic barbecues like the Kamado Joe.

Charcoals to avoid

- **Quick-light charcoal / lighter fluid:** The simple advice from me for this fuel type is – don't even go there! Often labelled as 'match light' or 'quick light', this type of charcoal is treated with a flammable chemical. It can impart an undesirable flavour to your food. In a ceramic barbecue, this aroma could remain in the pores of the ceramic for a very long time.
- **Instant-light briquettes:** These are soaked in lighter fluid and give off a chemical smell that hangs around in your food. Avoid, unless you're after that petrol-smoked flavour.
- **Unlabelled bulk charcoal:** If you don't know what's in it, don't burn it under your food.
- **Anything that doesn't say 'natural' in the title:** These will invariably have chemicals either for transport to prevent combustion or other nasties we don't want.
- **Charcoal with 'flavour enhancers':** These are often synthetic and unnecessary – stick to wood for your smoke.

Matching charcoal to your cook

COOK TYPE	FUEL RECOMMENDS
Searing steaks	Lump charcoal for high heat
Low and slow brisket	Briquettes with wood chunks
Kamado-style grilling	Lump charcoal for airflow control
Burgers and sausages	Either – go with what you've got
Portable/travel barbecues	Briquettes for longer stability

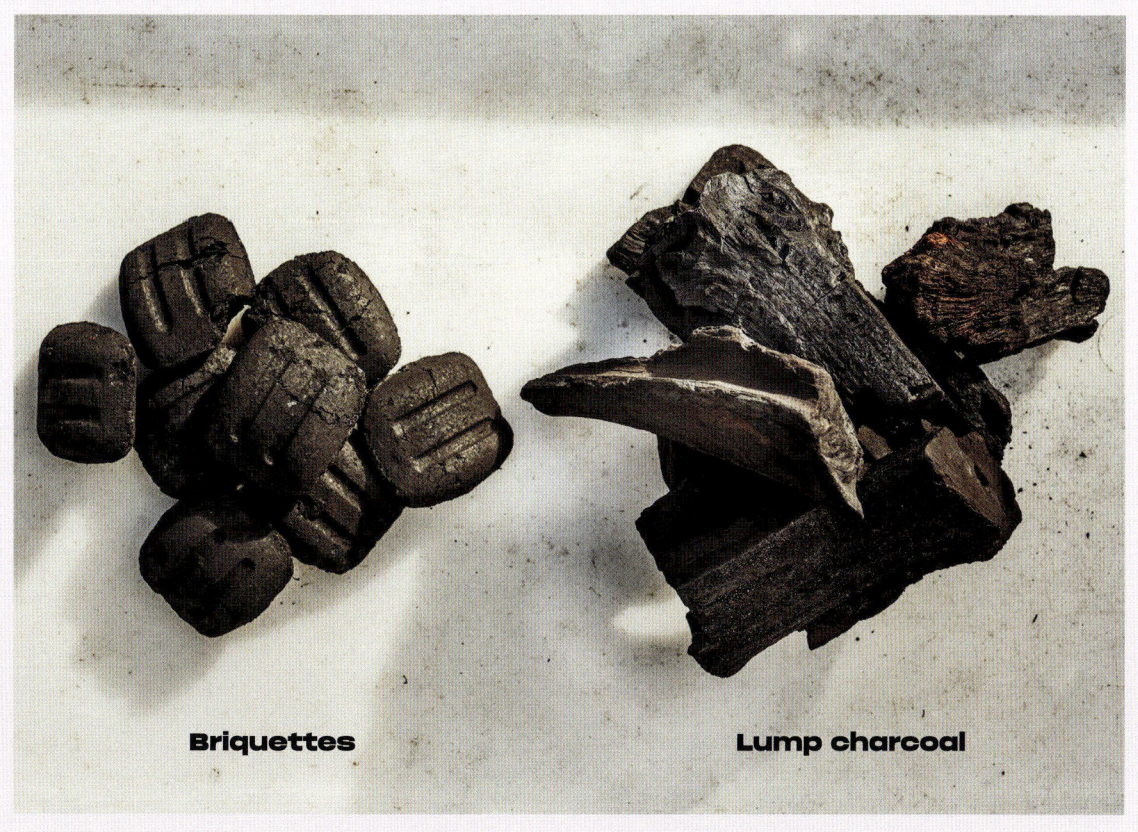

Briquettes   **Lump charcoal**

Pro tips for charcoal cooking

- **Build a two-zone fire:** (Direct and indirect) Hot side for searing, cooler side for finishing. Essential for control.

- **Use a chimney starter:** Skip the lighter fluid – get your coals roaring naturally in 15–20 minutes.

- **Top-up mid cook:** Add lump charcoal carefully during long cooks – it lights quicker and won't stall your fire.

- **Control the fire with air, not fuel:** Adjust vents, not charcoal piles, to dial in temperature.

- **Let it ash over?** This isn't required with natural charcoal; this was invariably the advice in years gone by, but it was more specially aimed at giving the coals time to burn off any chemicals. Don't cook until the coals are well established, but they don't have to be grey-white and glowing. We control our fire with oxygen and volume of fuel. We master the fire, we don't let the fire master us. In addition to the control methods for the fire we also have our zones – and remember, we may want to add more fuel as we go, if needed.

COMBINING CHARCOAL & WOOD

One of the best barbecue secrets? Layer lump charcoal with chunks of hardwood. You get the heat from the charcoal and the flavour from the wood, but you also get control and character, all in one cook.

If you're new to this, a great entry-level way into wood smoking is to combine lumps of wood with your charcoal cook. Here are a few of my favourite combinations:

→ OAK OR HICKORY + CHARCOAL = Brisket Magic

→ APPLEWOOD + CHARCOAL = Perfect Pork Chops

→ PECAN + CHARCOAL = Smoked Duck Gold

Using wood chunks with charcoal the barbecue

- **Ideal size of wood chunks?** Use fist-sized chunks (approximately 5–7.5cm/2–3in wide) when mixing wood with charcoal. Smaller chunks can burn too quickly; larger chunks may produce excessive smoke.

- **Best time to add wood chunks?** Add wood chunks just before placing food on the grill, when the charcoal is fully lit and burning steadily. This maximises smoke flavour, as raw meat absorbs smoke better at the beginning of the cook.

- **How many chunks for subtle flavour?** Using 1–2 fist-sized wood chunks will give a gentle, subtle smoke profile that's ideal for poultry, fish or vegetables. Using more than 3 chunks may overpower delicate meats.

- **Crucial tips for best results:**
  PLACEMENT: Position wood chunks directly on top of lit charcoal, evenly spaced out, to maintain consistent smoke.

  AVOID OVER-SMOKING: Too much smoke can add a bitter taste. Subtlety is key – less is often more.

  LID ON: Always grill with the lid closed, to retain smoke and flavour.

  SOAKING NOT REQUIRED: Wood chunks don't need soaking. Dry wood produces cleaner smoke.

  QUALITY MATTERS: Use hardwood chunks like oak, apple, cherry or hickory for the best flavour results.

FIRE LIGHTING & MANAGEMENT

Lighting the barbecue is a simple process. For a gas grill, ignite the burners you need, then simply turn the knob to increase or decrease the temperature.

For pellet grills, select your desired temperature and hit a button – the onboard fans, thermometer and computer all do the rest. Often, a signal sent to your mobile phone lets you know what's happening!

But for charcoal, it takes a little more involvement. I will break this down to cover two types of charcoal grills and explain why they are different. However, using either method will allow you to start any charcoal grill. Here's a guide to help you get started.

The two most common styles of charcoal grills in the home or backyard are **kettle grills** and **ceramic grills** shown below. First up is the trusty kettle grill. This is most often found in the 57" size, but other sizes are available too. My recipes and instructions focus primarily on the 57", as it is the most common.

Kettle Grill   **Ceramic Grill**

Kindling/firelighters

Choosing the proper kindling or fire lighter can expedite the process of heating your grill. I recommend using all-natural 'tumbleweeds', which are wax-coated wood shreds that look a little like mini pasta balls, or fire-starter cubes, which can be made entirely of wax or a combination of wax and wood or cardboard pulp. Both options burn cleanly with minimal ash.

Electric, hot air or gas lighters

While these grill lighters can be a bit on the expensive side, they allow you to light your charcoal fairly quickly without a chimney. The downside is that you need to remain nearby to keep the lighter on until the charcoal is fully ignited.

Charcoal chimney

My preferred method for igniting charcoal on a non-kamado-style grill is using a charcoal chimney. This device typically features a metal cylinder with air holes, a side handle and a grate at the bottom to hold the charcoal. Place it on the BBQ and fill to the top with charcoal, then place kindling or a natural firelighter underneath it before lighting it. This approach usually prepares your charcoal in about 10–15 minutes, roughly the same time it takes to preheat an oven. With natural charcoal, you don't need to wait until the charcoal has ashed over and gone grey. This is reserved for fuel that has been treated with chemicals. As you see the flames start to come out of the top of the chimney, it is good to go and can be emptied into your barbecue.

The chimney starter can be used to measure the barbecue. Check the instructions on your chimney starter/BBQ as they may differ in size.

HOW TO LIGHT A CERAMIC KAMADO-STYLE CHARCOAL GRILL

For ceramic kamado-style grills, I recommend using lumpwood charcoal. The main reason for this is the airflow. These grills are incredibly well insulated; as such, they rely on the constant airflow that comes from the bottom vent on the grill and exits via the top vent. Simply put, briquettes create a lot more ash when cooked, which can settle on the bottom of the grill and thus reduce or block that airflow, ultimately starving the fire of oxygen. Lumpwood charcoal won't create this issue.

You're ready to light your grill once you've selected your charcoal and gathered your tools. Follow these steps:

1. **PREPARE YOUR FIRE STARTER:** Place your preferred charcoal into the grill and bank it towards the rear. Underneath and at the bottom of the banked charcoal, ignite one or two tumbleweeds or natural fire-starter cubes.

2. **ALLOW THE CHARCOAL TO IGNITE:** The fire starter will gradually ignite the charcoal at the bottom, and with the fuel being banked and the air source being below and in front of the fuel, it will encourage the fire to move up and evenly ignite the rest from the bottom up. This process typically takes around 15 minutes. You'll quickly notice the smoke transition from thick white to thin blue, indicating that the charcoal is catching at this stage. When the charcoal has caught and started to establish, close the lid and open the top daisy wheel vent fully. This will accelerate the airflow through the grill, pulling air up from the bottom and assisting in the lighting process.

3. **LET THE CHARCOAL TAKE:** After 10 minutes, open the lid and, using a rake or other instrument, draw and distribute the lit charcoal across your grill. Using a heat-resistant glove, insert the cooking grates and close the lid again. Watch the lid temperature rise; when it is 20–30°C (68–86°F) from the desired temperature you wish to cook on, close the top vent to a quarter open. On the bottom vent, close this to a roughly one-finger-width gap. Your grill will then settle to your desired temperature.

4. **BRING IT TO TEMPERATURE:** Closing the grill lid will allow the lid to come to temperature and preheat. A kamado grill, by its ceramic nature, will also cook with radiant heat from the top down. This step is important when preparing your fire and achieving consistent heat.

5. **CONTROL THE TEMPERATURE:** To maintain a consistent temperature throughout the cook, adjust the bottom vent to allow more oxygen into the firebox. This is achieved primarily by manipulating the lower vent. Think of this vent as your 10, 20, 30°C (50, 68, 86°F) adjustment and the upper vents as your fine-tuning in 2–5°C (35–41°F). The top vent's main job is to pull the air from below and allow it to escape, similar to a chimney in your house, which pulls all the smoke up and out. More airflow increases heat, so opening the vents raises the temperature, while closing them lowers it.

6. **EXTINGUISH THE GRILL:** After cooking, it's a simple matter of cutting off the airflow to the grill. Close the lid and all vents, allowing the fire to extinguish naturally. It can take several hours for the coals to completely cool, so keep this in mind, and I would suggest not transferring and disposing of the ash until the next day or 24 hours later.

By following these tips, you'll be well on your way to successfully lighting your charcoal grill and enjoying a delicious barbecue.

CREATING ZONES

Creating zones in your BBQ is a great way to level-up and control your cooking, allowing you to experiment with different methods.
I implement the two-zone configuration on a grill to facilitate indirect cooking, which is far more gentle than direct heat cooking. Think of direct being like using your hob or stove top for searing, and the indirect side as your oven, where you would move food to after for roasting or finishing.

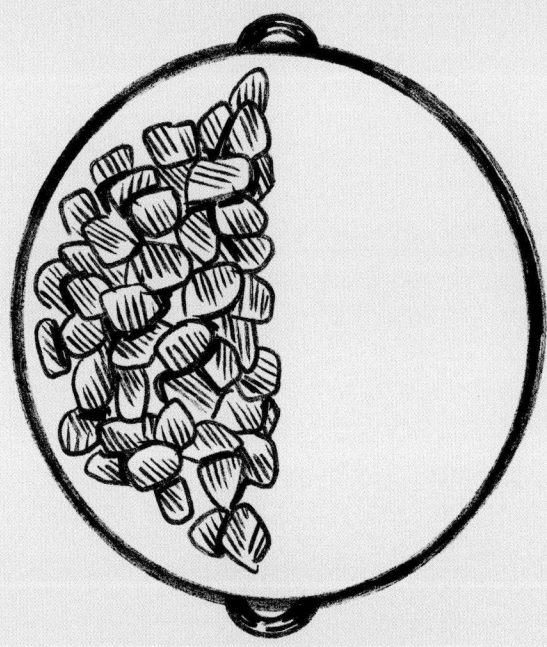

50/50 split of direct / indirect heat

The zone setup that I use for the vast majority of my cooking is on a **50/50 split of direct / indirect.**

Often, throughout this book, I mention moving the food to the indirect side. This is where most of our cooking is done on a barbecue.

Direct is the hot zone, directly over the coals, and is used to sear the meat at the beginning or end of the cooking process. This zone exposes the food immediately to high heat, which is ideal for quickly cooking smaller, thinner items like steaks, burgers and vegetables.

Indirect grilling is a barbecue technique where the food cooks next to, rather than directly over, the heat source, allowing for gentle, slow cooking, which is ideal for larger cuts or foods that require even internal cooking without excessive charring. Indirect grilling effectively turns your barbecue into an outdoor oven, perfect for foods that benefit from roasting or slow-cooking to tender, juicy perfection.

Once set up, the **two-zone configuration** creates both hotter and cooler zones within the same grill. Though it's most prominently used with charcoal grills, the two-zone set up is possible with gas grills, too.

Think of these zones as tools in your barbecue kit – adjustable, flexible and designed to help you take control of your cook. Using accessories like an ash tool or fire baskets, you can reconfigure your coals mid-cook to suit whatever's on the grill. The key is cooking with intention, not just heat.

EXPERIMENTING WITH GRILL SETUPS

Once you've mastered the 50/50 method you might want to experiment, so I've included a few others and what I would recommend you use them for.

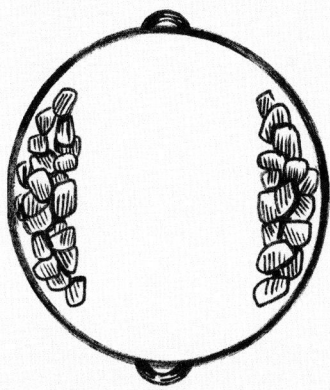

Two-sided

The two-sided configuration provides steady, indirect heat for slow, even cooking without burning the exterior.

Perfect for: larger cuts like whole chickens, roasts or a leg of lamb.

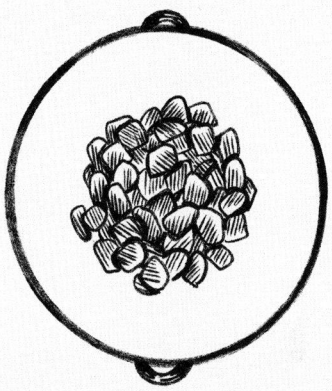

Pile

Used to create different heat zones for various cooking techniques.

Perfect for: foods like chicken wings or shell-on oysters, which benefit from gentle, indirect heat.

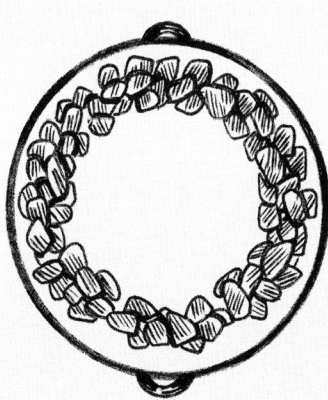

Ring of Fire

A great way to control vertical heat exposure.

Perfect for: beer-can chicken or Yorkshire puddings.

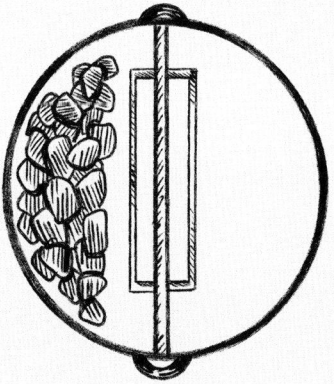

One-sided

This is built for rotisserie cooking.

Perfect for: shawarma, porchetta or any whole joints of meat – and the space below can be used to cook vegetables and catch the flavour-packed drippings in a tray.

All

Designed for fast direct cooking.

Perfect for: thinner cuts such as burgers, prawns, steaks or veg.

For a kettle charcoal grill

Light a chimney of coals and, once ready, pile them on one side of the grill, leaving the other side clear and empty. If you do not require direct heat at all, you may want to arrange the coals along the outside of the grill in a ring formation. This is particularly useful on the round kettle grill and will make the entire central zone indirect.

For a ceramic kamado-style grill

It's possible to replicate these zones. However, most kamado grills also come with some form of deflector plate, which is a more efficient method. When inserted, the deflector plate will, as the name suggests, deflect direct heat away from this area of the grill. You do need to be mindful that, if there is fuel directly under the deflector, it will then radiate heat.

Hence it's a good idea to bank the coals towards the direct side and have less under the deflector plate.

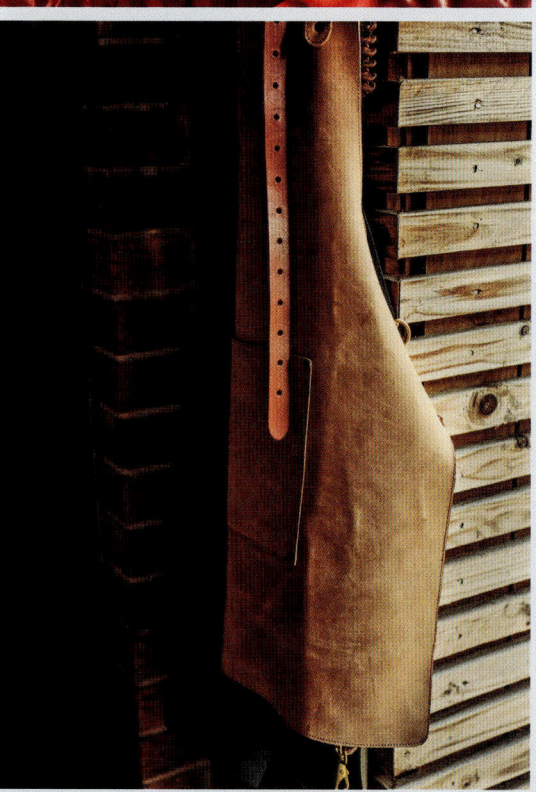

For a gas grill

Light both the end burners, leaving the middle burners off. For example, if you have a 4-burner grill, light the very left and very right burners, and consider the middle the indirect zone. This works well for roasting.

Alternatively, light the two left burners and leave the two right burners off. This works well for grilling large steaks and burgers, etc., allowing for a safe zone to move food to if you get flare-ups.

Zones can also apply in terms of height. If your grill allows it, you can set the cooking grates at different levels. For example, the divide and conquer system as seen in the Kamado Joe grills.

THE FIRE TRIANGLE

Before you even think about flipping a steak or slow-smoking a brisket, you've got to understand one of the most important principles in live-fire cooking: the fire triangle. Sounds technical, but it's very simple: every fire needs heat, fuel and oxygen. That's it. Take one away, and your fire's done for. However, if we control one or more of these elements, we can control the fire.

Whether you're firing up a kamado, kettle or offset smoker, knowing how to balance these three elements is the difference between a barbecue disaster and a backyard legend.

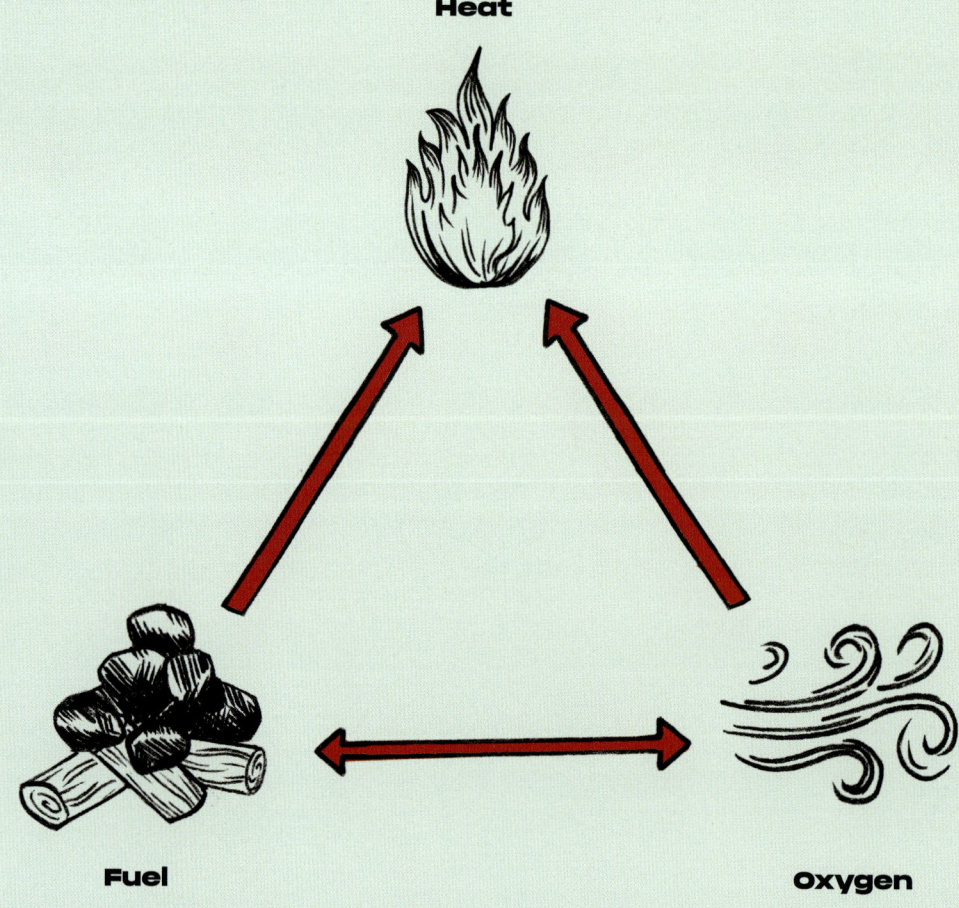

THE THREE SIDES OF THE FIRE TRIANGLE

HEAT
The spark that starts it all

You need heat to ignite your fuel. In barbecue terms, that's usually a chimney starter, firelighters or an electric igniter. Once the fire's going, heat becomes your cooking engine. Managing it means mastering how long to sear, how slow to smoke and how to nail that perfect pink smoke ring.

FUEL
The fire's main meal

This is what burns (see pages 12–14). Lumpwood charcoal, briquettes, hardwood chunks – they're all fuel. Each brings something different to the table. Briquettes burn longer and more evenly, perfect for long cooks. Lumpwood charcoal lights faster and burns hotter. Want extra flavour? Throw in some cherry or hickory wood.

But... This is the first element of the triangle that we can control: how much fuel we add into the fire from the outset or during the cook process, and the maximum temperature the fire can achieve.

OXYGEN
The invisible boss

No oxygen, no fire. It's that simple at a basic level. That's why your barbecue has vents – those little sliders or flaps control how much air gets in and out. More air = hotter fire. Less air = cooler or no fire. On a kettle or kamado barbecue, bottom vents feed the fire and top vents exhaust the smoke, in effect pulling the oxygen in from below. On a smoker, managing airflow is how you dial in low 'n' slow temperatures for hours.

This is the second element of the triangle that we can control. The first stage is to cook with the lid closed as much as possible. Leaving the lid open allows an unrestricted volume of oxygen into the fire, leading to rapidly rising temperatures. I often hear people at my classes and cooking demonstrations state that their barbecue gets too hot, so they open the lid to let the heat out. It may sound counterintuitive, but leaving the lid closed and controlling the bottom vent will actually bring the temperature down and help stabilise those spikes in the temperature.

Here's a real-world barbecue example. Let's say you're cooking a pork shoulder low and slow. You light your **fuel** (lumpwood charcoal) using a chimney starter (**heat**), and add a couple of cherry wood chunks for smoke. Then, you dial in the **oxygen** using your vents to keep the temperature steady at 120°C (250°F). Leave the vents wide open and it'll run hot; close them too much and the fire will choke out. Find that sweet spot and you're laughing.

Use the triangle, don't fight it

Most barbecue issues – crazy temperatures that get away from you, a weak fire without enough energy, bitter-tasting smoke spoiling the flavour of the food – can all be traced back to one side of the triangle being off or needing attention.

So next time, if things start to go sideways, ask yourself: *Do I have enough heat? Is my fuel right? Am I getting the airflow I need? Am I getting too much airflow?*

Master the fire triangle, and you're halfway to mastering your barbecue.

SEASONING & SMOKING

I'm always asked for the perfect barbecue recipe – for steak, chicken, whatever it may be. The truth is, there's no one single ideal recipe or approach to barbecuing. There are endless combinations and flavours to explore, so I've included my own personal flavour wheel that you can turn to when you want to experiment with the recipes I have shared here.

BARBECUE FLAVOUR PROFILE GUIDE

Use this guide to explore the seven key flavour profiles that will help you create perfectly balanced barbecue dishes, guaranteed to impress your guests. Experimenting with and tasting the ingredients below will let you discover new combinations, refine your recipes and elevate your grilling game.

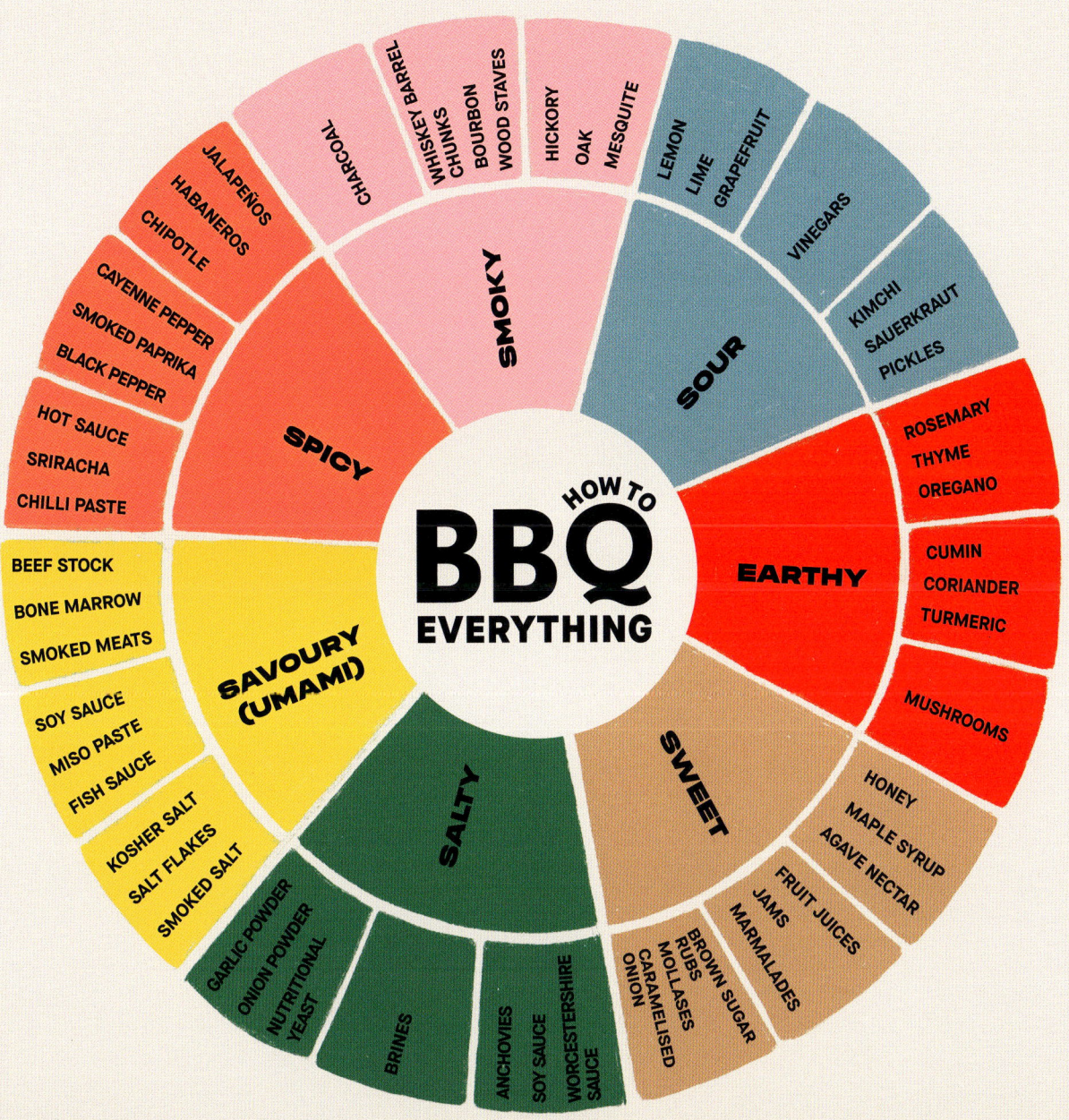

SEASONING & SMOKING

SMOKING WOODS
– THE SOUL OF BARBECUE

Barbecue isn't just about fire, it's about smoke. That curl of fragrant wood smoke drifting from your pit isn't just for show, it's flavour, it's seasoning, it's history, and it provides character.

Choosing the right smoking wood

Every wood has its own flavour profile. Some are mild and sweet, perfect for poultry and vegetables. Others are intense and bold, made for brisket or ribs. The key is matching the wood's strength to your ingredient. This chart below shows some smoking woods and food pairings for you. Remember, you can layer woods much like rubs. For example, with brisket you may want to use 2 parts oak and 1 part cherry. The oak delivers the flavour and the cherry adds some sweetness as well as some colour.

	APPLEWOOD	CHERRY	MAPLE	HICKORY	OAK	PECAN	ALDER	MESQUITE
Chicken	✓	✓	✓				✓	
Shrimp	✓		✓				✓	
Lamb					✓			
Pork	✓	✓	✓			✓		
Beef		✓		✓	✓			✓
Corn	✓					✓	✓	
Cheese		✓		✓		✓		

How to use smoking wood

- **Charcoal grills:** Toss one or two fist-sized wood chunks directly onto the hot coals. For longer cooks, use more chunks and bury them in the coals prior to lighting.

- **Gas grills:** Use a smoker box or foil pouch filled with chips. Place it over a lit burner on low.

- **Kamado and ceramic grills:** Add wood chunks as above to the charcoal for steady, even smoke. If you need to add extra mid-cook, place smaller chunks into the ash tray.

- **Pellet smokers:** Use the right pellets for your protein – fruit woods for poultry and pork, hardwoods for beef and game (see table).

CLEAN SMOKE VS DIRTY SMOKE
Know the difference – it can make or break your barbecue.

If you've ever had a barbecue that tasted acrid, bitter, or like licking a chimney, chances are it was hit with dirty smoke. It's one of the most common mistakes when using wood – and one of the easiest to fix once you know what to look (and smell) for.

Clean smoke
Appearance: Thin, wispy, almost blue or transparent.
Smell: Pleasant, sweet, woodsy.
Taste: Enhances the natural flavour of the meat without overpowering it.
Result: Bark forms beautifully, meat stays juicy and the smoke ring pops.

How to achieve it
- Use well-seasoned (dry but not dusty) hardwood.
- Ensure good airflow – smoke needs oxygen.
- Maintain stable temperatures and avoid overloading with wood.
- Let the fire breathe, don't smother it with too much fuel too quickly.

Dirty smoke
Appearance: Thick, white or grey plumes.
Smell: Acrid, sharp, chemical-like.
Taste: Bitter, burnt, unpleasant coating on the tongue.
Result: Blackened bark, dry or tough meat and a ruined cook.

What causes it
- Wet or green wood.
- Poor airflow and smouldering fires.
- Too much wood dumped onto an underdeveloped fire.
- Grease hitting open flames and creating smoke (particularly in offset smokers or kettles).

HOW TO PROPERLY APPLY A BARBECUE RUB

Using a barbecue rub isn't about physically rubbing it in, despite the name. The goal is to coat the meat evenly, enhance flavour and build a great bark (that beautiful crust we all chase on a proper low 'n' slow cook). Here's how to do it right:

Set up for success

- **Start by placing your meat in a large foil or metal tray.** Not only does this help contain the mess, but it also saves on wasted rub, especially if you're seasoning multiple racks of ribs or joints of meat. As long as it hasn't touched raw meat, any rub that falls can be reused for a second batch another day.

Choose your slather *(optional)*

- **If your meat surface is a little dry, you can use a light slather** – such as mustard, oil or hot sauce – to help the rub stick. But if the meat is already slightly tacky or moist, skip it. Less is more here, and sometimes it's not needed at all.

Apply from a height

- **Hold your rub in one hand and sprinkle it from 20–30cm (8–12in) above the meat.** This helps it fall evenly like rain, covering the surface without clumps or heavy patches. Go light at first, you can always add more, but you can't take it away.

Pat, don't rub

- **Once the rub is down, gently pat it into the surface with the flat of your hand.** You're not massaging a steak – just encouraging it to bond. Rubbing can smear your slather or create uneven seasoning. Pressing helps it stick, while keeping your flavour layers intact.

Don't forget the edges

- **Season all sides.** This seems obvious, but the edges are often missed and they're prime real estate for flavour – especially on ribs, chops or any meat with exposed sides. Tilt or rotate the meat in the tray and repeat the same process on every angle.

Layering rubs for depth and bark

- **For more complex flavour and a better bark, layering rubs can be a game changer.** Start with a fine base rub – something like SPG (salt, pepper, garlic) – to penetrate and season the meat evenly. Then follow up with a more textured, coarser rub on top to help build bark during the cook. Think of the total volume of rub you want on the meat and break it down into percentages. For example, a brisket might get 70 per cent SPG as the base, followed by 20 per cent extra freshly ground black pepper to enhance the bark and 10 per cent of a rub with a touch of heat, like a chilli blend. The key is balance – make sure the rubs complement each other and don't double up too heavily on the same salt or sugar levels. When used well, two or three well-matched rubs can bring depth without overpowering the meat.

Let it sit (if you can)

- **If time allows, let your meat sit for 20–30 minutes after rubbing, especially for larger cuts.** This gives the seasoning time to draw in moisture and start forming a light crust. It also helps the flavours bind better before the cook begins. Using your rub right is half the battle. Do it with care and consistency and you're already on the path to barbecue greatness.

RESTING MEAT

Resting meat is essential, and really the benefit of this cannot be underestimated. Have you ever sliced into a steak right after cooking only to see those precious juices escape onto your cutting board? This is exactly why resting is critical. When meat cooks, the tightly bundled protein fibres contract, pushing moisture to the edges. Resting allows these fibres to relax, enabling the juices to flow and evenly distribute throughout the meat.

A general rule of thumb is to allow the meat to rest for a quarter to a third of the overall cooking time. Generally, a quick-cooked item will benefit from a 10-minute rest, while a long roast like whole turkey, rib roast, etc., will benefit from 30–45 minutes or more.

When resting smaller cuts, simply placing them on a tray elevated on a wire rack, loosely covered in foil (not wrapped), will keep the food sufficiently warm to allow it to rest.

Larger cuts should be wrapped in foil and placed onto a tray to catch any escaping juices for gravy, etc. These can be wrapped or draped in a couple of towels or placed into a cooler.

Tip: Using something like a roto-moulded cooler like a Yeti, etc., means you can let the meat rest for several hours until you're ready to serve, and it is a great way to take any pressure out of preparing food for larger-gathering days, like summer parties and Christmas.

SLICING OR CARVING

How you slice your meat is vitally important. You may have heard of the term slicing or cutting against the grain. The grain refers to the direction of the muscle fibres, which are generally aligned in a single direction. I say normally, as they will change direction in the likes of tri-tip and full briskets. Slicing against the grain means slicing across the fibres and cutting the fibres into smaller cross-sections, which significantly improves the tenderness and overall enjoyment when eating.

The grain is often easier to see before cooking, so you can take a mental note, and the grain or fibre direction is more noticeable in the likes of sirloins, hanger, picanha, tri-tip, etc.

Tip: For other items, like brisket, when first starting out you can give yourself a cheat by placing a slightly exaggerated slice in the corner from which you will begin your slicing to show the path to follow. As the likes of brisket can change shape during cooking, this can make it a little easier.

STARTERS,
SIDES
& Sides
SIDES
STA

BACON-WRAPPED ONION RINGS

Crispy, sticky and made for BBQ glazing

Prep Time: 15 minutes

Cook Time: 45–60 minutes

SERVES 4–6

- 2 large cooking onions (e.g. Spanish or brown onions), cut into 2cm (¾in) thick rings
- 12–16 rashers of streaky bacon (smoked or unsmoked)
- Your favourite BBQ rub (see pages 224–9)
- BBQ sauce of choice (try the Magners BBQ sauce – see page 231)

These bacon-wrapped onion rings are smoky, sticky and seriously addictive. Thick-cut onion slices get wrapped in streaky bacon, then dusted with your favourite barbecue rub and slowly cooked over the coals until crisped and glazed. They're perfect as a barbecue side, a beer snack, or stacked high on a burger. Make a whole batch, as you'll never have enough.

Prep
Carefully separate the onion slices into whole rings (you can double up rings for extra structure, if needed). Discard the small inner rings or save for another use. Wrap each onion ring tightly with a rasher of bacon, slightly overlapping until the entire ring is covered. Place the wrapped rings on a wire rack or tray.

Dust the bacon-wrapped onion rings generously with your favourite BBQ rub on all sides. Let them rest for 10 minutes while you preheat your barbecue to temperature.

Prepare your barbecue for indirect cooking at 180–200°C (350–400°F). Place the rings on a rack or directly on the grill grates away from the coals.

Grill
Cook for 30–40 minutes, until the bacon begins to crisp. Start brushing with BBQ sauce every 15–20 minutes, turning as needed, until the bacon is fully cooked and the glaze is sticky and caramelised – the total cook time will be 45–60 minutes.

Serve
Remove from the grill and let them rest for a few minutes before serving. They're great on their own or as part of a bigger barbecue platter.

→ **Add Heat:** Mix dried chilli flakes or cayenne pepper into the rub or glaze for a spicy kick.
→ **Stuff It:** Fill the onion rings with cheese before wrapping, for a molten centre.
→ **Finish with Crunch:** Top with crispy fried onions or jalapeños just before serving.
→ **Serve With:** Ranch dressing, blue cheese dip or even more BBQ sauce on the side.
→ **Burger Upgrade:** Use one onion ring as a burger topper, for smoky crunch and drama.

BUFFALO CHICKEN POTATO SKINS

The ultimate BBQ starter

Prep Time: 20 minutes

Cook Time: 1 hour 20 minutes

SERVES 4–6

Ingredients
4 medium baking potatoes (such as Russet), scrubbed clean
Oil, for brushing
170g (6oz) hot sauce (I like Frank's RedHot)
2 tbsp butter, melted
450g (16oz) warm cooked chicken, shredded or diced
60g (2½oz) Cheddar, grated
60g (2½oz) blue cheese, crumbled
Sea salt and freshly ground black pepper

TO SERVE

2 spring onions, sliced
Celery and carrot sticks
55g (2oz) blue cheese dressing

These loaded potato skins are everything you want in a barbecue snack – crispy, spicy, cheesy and perfect for tearing into with your hands. A fiery mix of buffalo chicken fills golden potato shells, then gets topped with melted Cheddar and blue cheese for that unmistakable hot wing flavour. Finished with spring onions and served with cool blue cheese dressing, this dish is a guaranteed hit for game day, barbecue parties or laid-back weekends.

Prep

Preheat the oven to 200°C/180°C fan (400°F). Prick the potatoes with a fork and bake for about 1 hour, or until tender. Allow to cool slightly.

Cut each potato in half lengthwise and scoop out most of the flesh, leaving about 1cm (½in) of potato in the skin. (Save the scooped potato for mash or another recipe.) Brush the skins all over with oil.

In a bowl, mix the hot sauce with the melted butter, then toss in the warm chicken to coat evenly.

Preheat your barbecue for direct cooking at 230°C (450°F).

Grill

Place the skins cut-side down on the grill and cook for 10 minutes per side, or until golden and crispy.

Season the inside of the potato skins with a little salt and pepper. Fill with the buffalo chicken mixture and top with the Cheddar and blue cheese.

Place the filled potato skins back on the barbecue (indirect side works best here) and cook with the lid closed for 3–5 minutes, just until the cheese has melted.

Serve

Remove from the grill, sprinkle with sliced spring onions, and serve immediately with a side of celery and carrot sticks and some blue cheese dressing for dipping.

→ **Extra Heat:** Add sliced jalapeños or a drizzle of sriracha on top for spice lovers.

→ **BBQ Twist:** Stir in a little smoky BBQ sauce to the chicken for a buffalo-meets-barbecue fusion.

→ **Meat Swap:** Use pulled pork or grilled prawns instead of chicken for a different protein punch.

→ **Make It Mini:** Use baby potatoes for bite-sized party snacks or grazing boards.

→ **Herby Finish:** Garnish with chopped chives, parsley or coriander for a fresh contrast.

CRANBERRY & PARMA HAM TEAR & SHARE *with* BAKED CAMEMBERT

Twisted, gooey and built for sharing

Prep Time: 15 minutes

Cook Time: 20–25 minutes

SERVES 4–6

2 sheets of ready-rolled puff pastry
1 whole Camembert wheel
1 jar cranberry sauce
1 pack Parma ham slices
1 garlic clove, thinly sliced
A few sprigs of fresh rosemary
2 egg yolks, beaten
Grated Parmesan (optional)

This tear and share bake brings the wow factor to any barbecue or festive feast. A wheel of Camembert sits at the heart of twisted puff pastry fingers filled with sweet cranberry sauce and salty Parma ham. Studded with fresh rosemary and garlic, and finished golden from the grill, it's a hands-on crowd-pleaser made for diving into with friends.

Prep

Preheat your barbecue or oven to 200°C/180°C fan (400°F), set for indirect cooking. Line a barbecue-safe tray or baking sheet with parchment.

Unroll the first sheet of puff pastry and place the Camembert in the centre. Spread a generous layer of cranberry sauce in a ring around the cheese, about 5–8cm (2–3in) wider than the Camembert. Lay the Parma ham over the cranberry sauce in strips or slightly overlapping layers.

Place the second pastry sheet over the top to cover. Use a sharp knife to cut slits outward from the edge of the cheese to form pastry 'fingers'. Twist each finger a couple of times to show the filling.

Slice a few hash marks into the top of the Camembert and insert garlic slices and small rosemary sprigs into the cuts. Brush the entire pastry with beaten egg yolk. Sprinkle with grated Parmesan, if using.

Grill

Place on the barbecue over indirect heat and cook for 20–25 minutes, until the pastry is puffed and golden and the Camembert is melted and gooey in the centre.

Serve

Bring it straight to the table. Tear, dip and enjoy while hot.

➔ `Make It Spicy:` Add a little chilli jam or harissa alongside the cranberry for a sweet-heat contrast.

➔ `Cheese Swap:` Swap Camembert for Brie or a flavoured soft cheese wheel.

➔ `Garnish:` Finish with a drizzle of honey and a few thyme leaves for extra depth.

➔ `Serve With:` Pickles, olives or a sparkling drink for a complete starter board.

➔ `Make It Mini:` Cut into smaller rounds for individual portions – great for parties.

STARTERS & SIDES

BBQ SHOTGUN SHELLS

Bacon-wrapped, glazed and full of flavour

Prep Time: 25 minutes

Cook Time: 1 hour–1 hour 20 minutes

SERVES 4–6

- 500g (17oz) burger mince (beef or mixed)
- 12 dried cannelloni tubes
- 12 rashers of streaky bacon
- Your favourite BBQ rub (see pages 224–9)
- BBQ sauce, for glazing (see pages 231–4)

EXTRAS FOR THE MAIN FILLING (optional)

- Fresh herb or spice blends (e.g. taco seasoning or Cajun mix)
- Grated Cheddar or mozzarella
- Cream cheese
- Finely chopped chillies
- Diced onions or garlic

Smoky, meaty and downright irresistible, these BBQ Shotgun Shells are one of those dishes that gets everyone talking. Cannelloni tubes stuffed with seasoned mince, then wrapped in streaky bacon and finished with a sticky glaze. The pasta softens as it cooks inside the bacon, locking in flavour and moisture. They're perfect as a barbecue snack, main or showpiece on a sharing platter.

Prep

In a bowl, mix the burger mince with your choice of BBQ rub or a shop-bought version and your favourite optional extras – whatever suits your taste, just make sure it can be tightly packed.

Using your fingers or a piping bag, firmly pack the meat filling into the uncooked cannelloni tubes from both ends until fully stuffed. Wrap each filled tube with a rasher of streaky bacon, overlapping slightly to fully encase the shell. Place seam-side down on a wire rack. Lightly dust with your favourite BBQ rub to build flavour as it cooks.

Set your barbecue for indirect cooking at 180–200°C (350–400°F). Place the rack over the indirect heat.

Grill

Cook on the rack for 45–60 minutes, or until the bacon is starting to crisp and the pasta has softened. Begin brushing with BBQ sauce every 5 minutes for 15–20 minutes, turning gently until the bacon is caramelised, sticky and crisped to perfection.

Serve

Rest for a few minutes, then slice or serve whole. These work brilliantly with slaw, pickles or dipping sauces on the side.

➔ **Add a Cheese Pull:** Insert a cheese stick or block of mozzarella into the middle of the filling before wrapping the cannelloni tubes.

➔ **Meat Swap:** Try pork sausage meat, lamb mince or spicy chorizo mixes.

➔ **Go Tex-Mex:** Add taco seasoning, jalapeños and grated cheese – serve with guac or soured cream.

➔ **Crunch Factor:** Dust the finished shells with crushed nachos or fried onions before serving.

➔ **Make It Mini:** Cut tubes in half for bite-sized party portions.

WATERMELON SALAD with FETA & OLIVES

Clean, cool and salty-sweet, built for grill days

Prep Time: 20 minutes, plus 20 minutes marinating

SERVES 6–8

- 1 seedless watermelon, skin removed and flesh cut into 4cm (1½in) chunks
- 120ml (4fl oz) spiced rum
- 4 cucumbers, cut into 4cm (1½in) chunks
- 450g (1lb) feta, crumbled
- 130g (4½oz) pitted olives
- 60ml (2½fl oz) extra virgin olive oil
- Small bunch of fresh oregano or flat-leaf parsley
- Sea salt and freshly ground black pepper

This one's a firm favourite when the sun's out and the grill's fired up. Fusing elements of the salty-sweet salads in the Caribbean and Mediterranean, I'd usually serve this alongside grilled jerk chicken or barbecue pork – this version swaps the usual citrus hit for a splash of spiced rum. It's light, colourful and full of contrast: sweet watermelon, briny olives, creamy feta and a subtle boozy bite.

Perfect as a side, or serve it as a bold centrepiece starter to get everyone talking.

Prep
Place the watermelon cubes in a large bowl. Pour over the rum and gently toss to coat. Set aside to marinate for about 20 minutes while you prep the rest.

Add the cucumber chunks to the watermelon along with the feta and olives, then drizzle over the olive oil. Season with salt and pepper to taste.

Serve
Gently toss everything together and pile it onto a large platter. Finish with a scattering of fresh oregano or parsley.

→ **Add Crunch:** Scatter over a handful of toasted pine nuts or crushed pistachios for texture.
→ **Spicy Kick:** Sprinkle with a pinch of dried chilli flakes.
→ **Citrus Swap:** Use a splash of lime zest and juice instead of rum for a booze-free version.

SMOKY JALAPEÑO BACON POPPERS *with* BBQ CREAM CHEESE

Smoky, spicy and downright moreish

Prep Time: 20 minutes

Cook Time: 20–25 minutes

Equipment: Cocktail sticks (optional, for securing)

SERVES 4

- 250g (9oz) cream cheese, softened
- 1 tbsp BBQ rub (see pages 224–9) or paprika
- ¼ tsp garlic powder
- 20 jalapeños, deseeded and cut in half
- 10 rashers of streaky bacon, cut in half
- Freshly ground black pepper

There's something about these fiery little mouthfuls that instantly takes me back to my early days in barbecue. I love jalapeños, they are practically their own food group, and wrapping them in bacon just brings them to another level. Spicy, smoky and stuffed with a silky, barbecue-spiced cream cheese. Trust me: make more than you think you'll need, as they vanish quicker than a cold beer on a hot day.

Prep

Get your grill ready for indirect cooking at a medium heat – you're aiming for around 160°C (325°F).

In a bowl, mix the softened cream cheese with your BBQ rub or paprika, garlic powder, and a generous crack of black pepper. You want it bold and punchy.

Spoon the cheese mixture into each jalapeño half – don't overfill, add just enough that it sits level with the top.

Wrap each one in half a strip of bacon, stretching it slightly as you go. If needed, pin them with a cocktail stick to hold everything in place.

Grill

Place the poppers onto a grill-safe tray or directly onto the cooler side of the barbecue. Close the lid and cook for 20–25 minutes, giving them a gentle turn once or twice until the bacon is crisp and the peppers have softened.

Serve

Lift the jalapeños off the grill and let them sit for a few minutes (they'll be molten inside). Serve warm with cold drinks and absolutely no regrets.

→ **Sweet & Heat:** Add a drizzle of hot honey over the finished poppers.
→ **Blue Cheese Bombs:** Swap cream cheese for a mix of blue cheese and crème fraîche.
→ **Fully Loaded:** Fold some crumbled sausage or pulled pork into the cream cheese for a meaty upgrade.

CRISP CUCUMBER & FENNEL SALAD

A fresh fix for rich BBQ fare

Prep Time: 15 minutes, plus 4-5 hours or overnight marinating

SERVES 6–8 AS A SIDE

500g (17oz) cucumber, thinly sliced (unpeeled but deseeded)

2 tbsp finely chopped fresh fennel

3 small white onions, very thinly sliced

175g (6oz) granulated sugar

1 tbsp sea salt

120ml (4fl oz) cider vinegar

This salad reminds me of warm afternoons exploring roadside barbecue joints in rural America, where every plate came with something pickled, sweet and zingy on the side. It's that crunch-and-tang combo that cuts through smoky meat and resets your palate between bites.

Here, I've taken that idea and freshened it up with thin cucumber slices, crisp onion and the delicate aniseed hit of fennel. A cider vinegar syrup pulls it all together – sweet, sharp and utterly refreshing. Serve it with pork, brisket or anything sticky off the grill. It's simple, clean and just what your barbecue platter needs.

Prep

Toss the sliced cucumber, fennel and onions together in a large bowl.

In a small bowl, combine the sugar, salt and cider vinegar. Stir until the sugar dissolves. Pour the syrup over the cucumber salad. Combine gently to coat everything evenly.

Cover tightly and chill for 4–5 hours, or up to 24 hours, to let the flavours mingle.

Serve

Serve cold or at room temperature. It will keep for 1 week in the fridge.

→ **Turn Up the Heat:** Add a few dried chilli flakes or thinly sliced fresh red chilli for heat.

→ **The Gentle Touch:** Swap cider vinegar for rice wine vinegar for a lighter, more delicate finish.

→ **Make It Punchy:** Stir in a few crushed coriander seeds or fennel seeds for extra aromatic punch.

MAC & CHEESE with TAYTO TOPPING

Smoky, spicy and seriously indulgent

Prep Time: 25 minutes

Cook Time: 25–30 minutes

SERVES 6–8

- 75g (3oz) unsalted butter, plus extra for greasing
- 3 mixed peppers (red/yellow)
- 40g (1½oz) plain flour
- 750ml (1¼ pints) whole milk, heated
- 500g (17oz) macaroni pasta
- 450g (1lb) mature Cheddar, grated, plus extra for topping
- Additional cheeses to taste (mozzarella, Gruyère, blue cheese all work brilliantly), grated or crumbled
- 4 chillies, finely chopped
- 1 tbsp hot sauce (adjust to taste)
- 1½ tsp kosher or sea salt
- ½ tsp freshly ground black pepper
- 1 bag of Tayto Rough Cuts Cheese & Onion crisps, crushed slightly

This is no ordinary mac and cheese. Loaded with melted Cheddar, roasted peppers and just the right amount of chilli heat, this barbecue-baked version is topped with crushed Tayto Rough Cuts Cheese & Onion crisps for extra crunch and savoury punch. It's rich, gooey and unapologetically over-the-top – just how comfort food should be. Perfect for feeding a crowd, especially when you want a side dish that steals the show.

Prep

Set up your barbecue for indirect cooking at 180–230°C (350–450°F). If using an oven, preheat to 200°C/180°C fan (400°F). Grease a large cast-iron skillet or baking dish with butter.

Grill the peppers whole over direct heat until the skins are blackened and blistered. Place in a bowl and cover tightly with cling film for a few minutes. Once cool, peel off the skins, deseed and chop into 1cm (½in) pieces.

In a large saucepan, melt the butter. Whisk in the flour and cook for 1 minute to form a roux. Gradually add the hot milk, whisking constantly until thickened and smooth. Remove from the heat.

Bring a large pot of salted water to the boil and cook the macaroni for about 2 minutes. You want it slightly underdone as it'll continue to cook on the BBQ. Drain well but don't rinse – the starch helps the sauce cling. If you're not using it straight away, toss it with a little butter or oil to stop it sticking together.

Stir in most of the Cheddar gradually until melted, followed by any additional cheeses. Once the sauce is smooth and gooey, stir in the chillies, roasted peppers, hot sauce, salt and pepper.

Fold the cheese sauce through the cooked macaroni until evenly coated. Pour into your prepared skillet or dish.

Grill

Cook over indirect heat on the barbecue (or in the oven) until bubbling at the edges – about 20 minutes. Once bubbling, top with crushed Tayto crisps and another light sprinkle of cheese.

Serve

Return to the barbecue/oven and cook for another 5–10 minutes, or until the top is golden, crisp and irresistible. Serve hot, straight from the pan.

→ **Add Protein:** Stir through crispy bacon, pulled pork or leftover brisket for a heartier dish.
→ **Turn Up the Heat:** Use hot smoked paprika, chipotle flakes or extra hot sauce for more punch.
→ **No Tayto?** Use kettle-cooked crisps or crushed crackers as a topping substitute.

CHARRED CORN, AVOCADO & SMOKED LIME SALAD

Bright, smoky and fresh

 Prep Time: 20 minutes

 **Cook Time:** 10–15 minutes

SERVES 4

- 2 corn cobs, husks removed, or 500g (17oz) tinned sweetcorn, drained
- 1 red pepper
- 1 tbsp olive oil
- 2 limes
- 1 ripe avocado, diced into 1cm (½in) cubes
- 300g (10oz) cherry tomatoes, cut in half
- 1 small red onion, finely chopped
- Small handful of fresh flat-leaf parsley and coriander, chopped
- Sea salt and freshly ground black pepper

FOR THE DRESSING

- Zest and juice of 1 lime
- 1 tsp runny honey
- ½ tsp smoked paprika
- ½ tsp ground cumin
- 1 tbsp olive oil

Charred corn and creamy avocado tossed with a zesty smoked-lime kick. This is sunshine in a bowl, with smoky grilled corn, creamy avocado and juicy cherry tomatoes brought together with a honey-lime dressing that's got just enough paprika to sing barbecue! We char a red pepper alongside the corn for a little extra sweetness and colour. Serve it with grilled meats, tacos or as a side to anything off the coals.

Prep

Get your barbecue running at medium-high heat (200–230°C/400–450°F) for direct cooking.

Brush the corn cobs and red pepper with a little of the olive oil and season lightly with salt and pepper.

In a small bowl, make the dressing by whisking together the lime zest and juice, honey, smoked paprika, cumin and olive oil. Season to taste.

Grill

Grill the corn and pepper directly, turning every few minutes until the corn is blistered and the pepper has softened and its skin has charred (10–15 minutes). If using tinned corn, sear the corn in a hot cast-iron skillet over the barbecue until charred. Set aside to cool. Cut the limes in half and grill flesh-side down on the BBQ until blackened.

Serve

Slice the corn kernels off the cobs and deseed and dice the grilled red pepper. Add both to a large bowl along with the avocado, cherry tomatoes, red onion and herbs. Squeeze the chargrilled limes into the dressing, then pour into the bowl and toss gently to combine. Taste and adjust seasoning with more lime, salt or honey as needed.

➔ **Add Crunch:** Toss in a handful of crushed tortilla chips just before serving.

➔ **Make It Creamy:** Crumble over feta or queso fresco.

➔ **Turn It Into A Main:** Add grilled prawns, chicken or halloumi skewers and serve warm.

➔ **Kick It Up:** Stir through some finely chopped chilli or a splash of jalapeño hot sauce.

JALAPEÑO CORNBREAD
Golden, buttery and BBQ-ready

Prep Time: 10 minutes

Cook Time: 25 minutes

SERVES 8–10

50g (2oz) unsalted butter, melted, plus extra for greasing
225g (8oz) fine polenta
140g (5oz) plain flour
1 tbsp sugar
2 tsp baking powder
1½ tsp salt
2 × 284ml (9½fl oz) cartons buttermilk
2 eggs
Jalapeños, thinly sliced, for topping

Golden, smoky and spiked with jalapeños, this cornbread is a must alongside barbecued fried chicken or anything saucy off the grill. Cooked over indirect heat in a cast-iron pan, the cornbread develops a crisp crust and soft crumb inside. Buttermilk gives it that classic tang, while a touch of melted butter keeps it rich. Simple, satisfying and perfect for soaking up bold barbecue flavours.

Prep
Set up your barbecue for indirect cooking and heat to 220–230°C (425–450°F). Grease a cast-iron skillet or baking tin with a generous amount of butter.

In a large mixing bowl, combine the cornmeal, flour, sugar, baking powder and salt. In a separate bowl, beat together the buttermilk and eggs.

Pour the wet ingredients into the dry ingredients and stir until just combined. Add the melted butter and mix again gently. Do not overmix – you want a slightly lumpy, thick batter. Pour the batter into the prepared pan and smooth the top. Decorate with sliced jalapeños.

Grill
Place the pan onto the barbecue over indirect heat, close the lid, and bake for 25 minutes, or until golden and a skewer inserted into the centre comes out clean.

Serve
Let cool slightly before slicing. Serve warm as a side with chilli, BBQ pulled pork, fried chicken or as part of a sharing platter.

→ **Add Cheese:** Fold a handful of grated Cheddar or crumbled feta into the batter.

→ **Make It Smoky:** Add a teaspoon of smoked paprika or a pinch of dried chilli flakes for extra depth.

→ **Sweeten It Up:** Increase the sugar to 2-3 tablespoons for a sweeter cornbread, which is great with honey butter.

→ **Add Texture:** Stir in corn kernels or chopped spring onions for added bite.

→ **Serve With:** Butter, hot sauce or a drizzle of honey for contrasting flavour finishes.

CHEDDAR & BACON CORNBREAD

The ultimate BBQ sidekick

ADD TO THE BASE RECIPE:

115g (4oz) mature Cheddar, grated
4 rashers of streaky bacon, cooked until crispy, then chopped
1 tsp smoked paprika or a dash of hot sauce (optional)

How to Use It:
Fold the cheese and bacon through the batter just before pouring it into the hot pan. Top with an extra sprinkle of cheese if you're feeling bold.

Serve with ribs or brisket for a total flavour bomb.

CHEESY JALAPEÑO CORNBREAD

The very best spicy-savoury hit

ADD TO THE BASE RECIPE:

1–2 jalapeños, finely sliced (deseed if you prefer less heat)
60g (2½oz) grated Cheddar or Monterey Jack for extra ooze (optional)
1 tbsp chopped fresh coriander or spring onions (optional)

How to Use It:
Stir into the batter and save a few jalapeño slices to press onto the top before baking – it looks great and adds a little charred bite.

Perfect with shakshuka, chilli or pulled chicken.

SWEET MAPLE CORNBREAD

For breakfast or dessert

CHANGE THE BASE RECIPE:
Swap honey/sugar for 3 tablespoons of maple syrup, add ½ teaspoon of ground cinnamon and a handful of blueberries or chopped pecans, if you like.

How to Use It:
Serve warm with a pat of butter and a drizzle of extra maple syrup. Epic alongside coffee in the morning or as a sweet barbecue treat at the end of the night.

TABBOULEH

A bright, classic salad with a little grill-kissed addition

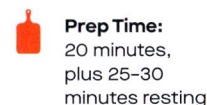

Prep Time: 20 minutes, plus 25–30 minutes resting

Bright, herb-packed tabbouleh built with fine bulgur, sharp lemon and good olive oil. Pile it beside grilled chicken or lamb, scoop into flatbreads, and char the lemons for a hint of smoke.

SERVES 4–6 AS A SIDE

- 90g (3½oz) fine bulgur
- 3 firm vine tomatoes, deseeded and finely diced (or use 2 tomatoes to dice and 1 to char; see method)
- ½ small cucumber, deseeded and finely diced (optional)
- 4 spring onions, very finely sliced
- 150–180g (5–6oz) fresh flat-leaf parsley, very finely chopped, thick stems removed
- 20–25g (¾–1oz) fresh mint, finely chopped

FOR THE DRESSING

- 2 lemons, halved (to char, if you like)
- 80ml (3fl oz) extra virgin olive oil
- 1 tsp fine sea salt, plus extra to taste
- ½ tsp ground allspice or 1 tsp sumac
- Freshly ground black pepper

TO GARNISH (OPTIONAL)

- Pinch of sumac
- Handful of pomegranate seeds

Prep
Over a medium-high heat place the lemon halves cut-side down for 2–3 minutes until lightly caramelised. If using, char one tomato the same way, then peel, deseed and dice.

Juice the lemons into a large bowl and strain out the pips. You want about 80ml (3fl oz). Add the salt and whisk in the olive oil, allspice or sumac, and a few grinds of pepper. Tip in the bulgur and stir well so every grain is coated. Rest for 15–20 minutes, stirring once or twice, until the grains are tender. If still a touch firm, add a tablespoon or two of hot water and rest a few minutes more.

Fold in the diced tomatoes (and the charred tomato, if using), cucumber if using, spring onions, parsley and mint. Toss until everything looks evenly green and glossy. Taste and adjust with more salt, pepper and lemon juice.

Serve
Rest for 10 minutes so the flavours settle. Serve cool or at room temperature, finished with a pinch of sumac and pomegranate seeds, if you like.

BBQ BEER ROLLS
Soft, fluffy, fireside rolls with a hit of lager

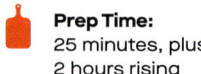

Prep Time:
25 minutes, plus 2 hours rising

Cook Time:
18–20 minutes

MAKES 14 ROLLS

| 105g (4oz) unsalted butter |
| 1 tbsp honey |
| 240ml (8fl oz) lager-style beer (something easy-drinking) |
| 2¼ tsp instant dried yeast (1 packet) |
| 465g (12½oz) plain flour, plus extra for dusting |
| 1 large egg, lightly beaten |
| 1½ tsp kosher salt |
| Salted butter, to serve |

These barbecue-friendly rolls are a staple at our house, especially when there's something rich and saucy on the grill – think bourbon ribs, pulled pork or anything begging to be mopped up.

They're soft, slightly sweet and get a little edge from the beer in the dough, making them ideal for cookouts or laidback weekend spreads.

Don't be put off by the yeast, these are simple to throw together and can be baked in a barbecue with a lid (a kamado-style grill is perfect for these) or in a home oven. Either way, they're best served warm, brushed with melted butter, and passed around with whatever smoky main is on the go.

Prep
In a small saucepan, melt 90g (3½oz) of the butter with the honey over low heat. Stir in the beer and warm the mixture to 38–46°C (100–114°F). (Use a thermometer if you've got one – if it's too hot it will kill the yeast.)

Pour the warm beer mix into a large bowl or stand mixer bowl. Stir in the yeast and let it sit for 5 minutes until slightly foamy. Add the flour, beaten egg and salt. Mix and knead until you've got a soft, slightly sticky dough – 5 minutes with a mixer, roughly 10 minutes by hand.

For the first rise, form the dough into a ball, cover the bowl with a clean towel or cling film, and let it rise in a warm spot for about 1 hour, or until doubled in size.

Turn the dough out onto a floured surface. Divide into 14 equal pieces (about 60g (2oz) each), roll into balls and place close together, but not touching, on a parchment-lined baking sheet.

For the second rise, cover loosely with cling film and let rise again until puffy, about 1 hour.

Preheat your oven or barbecue to 190°C (375°F).

Grill
Bake the rolls for 18–20 minutes, or until golden brown on top.

Serve
Melt the remaining butter and brush it over the hot rolls. Serve warm with salted butter.

➔ **Smoky twist?** Add a pinch of smoked salt or brush the tops with melted butter infused with roasted garlic or charred rosemary.

BBQ CRISPY POTATO SALAD *with* MUSTARD-CAPER DRESSING

Golden smashed spuds kissed by flame

Prep Time: 15 minutes, plus cooling

Cook Time: 30–40 minutes

SERVES 4–6

FOR THE POTATOES
- 750g (1½lb) baby potatoes
- 1 tbsp olive oil, plus extra for greasing (optional)
- 1 tsp smoked paprika
- Sea salt and freshly ground black pepper
- Small pinch of dried chilli flakes (optional, for heat), to serve

FOR THE DRESSING
- 3 tbsp mayonnaise
- 2 tbsp Greek-style yoghurt
- 1 garlic clove, finely grated
- 1 tbsp capers, drained and finely chopped
- 1 tsp Dijon mustard
- Zest and juice of ½ lemon
- 5 spring onions, thinly sliced
- 30g (1oz) fresh flat-leaf parsley, finely chopped

There's something about crispy potatoes and smoky barbecue flavour that just works, especially when it's all finished off with a tangy, herby sauce that cuts through the richness. This one was inspired by a simple tapas-style potato dish I had in a local restaurant here in Belfast, but with a full-blown barbecue twist. Instead of roasting, we crisp the smashed baby potatoes directly over the coals or in a hot griddle pan, giving them that fire-charred edge. The dressing brings everything together – creamy, lemony and packed with capers, mustard, garlic and herbs.

Prep
Add the potatoes to a saucepan of salted cold water and bring to the boil.

Simmer for 20–25 minutes until fork tender. Drain and let them steam-dry in the colander for a minute or two.

Place the potatoes on a tray or chopping board and gently press each one with the bottom of a glass or metal cup to flatten, aim for 1–1.5cm (½in) thick. Let them cool slightly to firm up.

While the potatoes are cooling slightly, stir together the mayo, yoghurt, garlic, capers, mustard, lemon zest and juice, half the spring onions and half the parsley. Taste and adjust seasoning as needed, adding a touch more lemon if you like it extra zippy.

Preheat your barbecue for direct heat (medium-high 180–230°C/350–450°F). Brush the potatoes lightly with olive oil and season with smoked paprika, salt and pepper.

Grill
Grill the smashed potatoes directly on the grates or a griddle, turning occasionally until crispy and golden on the edges, 10–15 minutes depending on heat. Watch for flare-ups and move them to a cooler zone if needed. Once crisp, transfer to a baking tray and let them cool for 5 minutes.

Serve
Lightly toss the grilled potatoes with half the dressing until just coated, then pile them up on a platter. Spoon over the remaining dressing and scatter with the remaining parsley and spring onions. Finish with a crack of black pepper and maybe a few chilli flakes if you're feeling bold.

Serve warm or at room temperature with grilled chicken, ribs or just a cold cider in hand.

KG EGYPTIAN-INSPIRED SALAD

Fresh, bright and BBQ-ready

Prep Time:
10 minutes

SERVES 4–6 AS A SIDE

- 2 cucumbers, diced
- 3 heirloom tomatoes (or other firm tomatoes), diced
- ½ medium red or yellow onion, finely diced
- Handful of fresh parsley leaves and soft stems, finely chopped
- Juice of 1 lemon
- 2 tbsp olive oil
- Sea salt and freshly ground black pepper
- Ground cumin, sumac, Aleppo pepper or cayenne pepper, to taste (optional)

Inspired by a visit to KG BBQ in Austin, Texas, this is my take on the salad that stole the show on the sides as a vibrant, refreshing dish to accompany the smoked meats. Crisp cucumber, juicy tomatoes, sharp onion and parsley are dressed simply in lemon juice and olive oil, seasoned generously with salt and optionally lifted with cumin, sumac or some gentle heat of Aleppo or cayenne pepper. It's the kind of side that makes barbecue mains sing and adds a bright contrast to the plate.

Prep

Place the cucumbers, tomatoes, onion and parsley in a bowl and add the lemon juice and olive oil directly – no need to mix the dressing separately. Add salt and pepper to taste. Don't be shy with the salt – it brings out the acidity of the lemon and ties the whole salad together.

For extra flavour, add a pinch or two of cumin, sumac, Aleppo pepper or cayenne – one or two at most to keep the flavours fresh and balanced.

Serve

Best served fresh alongside grilled meats, flatbreads or as part of a mixed mezze spread.

- ➜ **Bulk It Out:** Add diced avocado, chickpeas or grilled halloumi.
- ➜ **Chill It First**: Let it sit in the fridge for 15-30 minutes before serving, to let the flavours marry.
- ➜ **Pair It With:** Smoked lamb shoulder, koftas or harissa-grilled chicken.
- ➜ **Zingy Twist**: Add a dash of pomegranate molasses for extra tang and sweetness.

GARLIC BUTTER & PARMESAN-CRUSTED HASSELBACK POTATOES

Golden, crisp and packed with flavour

 Prep Time: 15 minutes, plus 10 minutes soaking (optional)

 Cook Time: 60–65 minutes

 Equipment: Wooden spoons or chopsticks

SERVES 4

- 4 large floury potatoes (such as Maris Piper or Russet)
- 100g (3½oz) unsalted butter, melted
- 2 tbsp olive oil
- 3 garlic cloves, finely minced
- 2 tbsp fresh parsley, finely chopped, plus extra to garnish
- 1 tsp sea salt
- ½ tsp freshly ground black pepper
- 50g (2oz) Parmesan, grated, plus extra to garnish
- 1 tbsp panko breadcrumbs (optional, for extra crunch)
- A drizzle of truffle oil (optional)

These Hasselbacks look impressive, but they're easier than you'd think. The thin slices soak up all the buttery garlic and herb flavour, while the Parmesan forms a golden crust across the top. They're the posh cousin to your usual roastie.

Prep

Set your oven (or barbecue with lid down, indirect heat) to 200°C/180°C fan (400°F).

Hold a potato between the handles of two wooden spoons or chopsticks. Slice thin slits across the potato, stopping when your knife hits the spoon handles or chopsticks – this keeps the base intact. Aim for slices about 3mm (⅛in) apart. (You can soak the sliced potatoes in cold water for 10 minutes to remove excess starch, which helps them fan out more easily when roasting. Just dry them well after.)

In a small bowl, combine the melted butter, olive oil, garlic, chopped parsley, salt and pepper. Brush the garlic butter generously over and into the slits of each potato. Place on a baking tray or in a cast-iron skillet.

Cook

Cook, uncovered, on the barbecue with the lid down or in the oven for 45 minutes, basting with more butter halfway through. After 45 minutes, remove the tray. The slices should be starting to fan open and the edges turning golden. Sprinkle the grated Parmesan (and the panko breadcrumbs, if using) over the tops, letting some fall between the slices. Return to the barbecue or oven for 15–20 minutes more, until crispy and golden.

Serve

Transfer to a platter or serve straight from the tray. Spoon over any garlicky butter left in the pan and finish with extra parsley, a touch more Parmesan, or even a drizzle of truffle oil if you're feeling fancy.

→ **Add Heat:** Add a sprinkle of smoked paprika or dried chilli flakes before baking.
→ **Cheesy Hit:** Swap Parmesan for grated aged Cheddar or Gruyère for a richer flavour.
→ **Hint of Herbs:** Add fresh thyme or rosemary to the garlic butter.

SALT & CHILLI BBQ WEDGES

The ultimate crispy sidekick

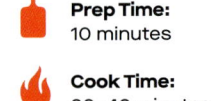

Prep Time: 10 minutes

Cook Time: 30–40 minutes

SERVES 4

- 4 large floury potatoes (Maris Piper or Russet work well), baked or raw
- 2 tbsp rapeseed or vegetable oil
- 1 tsp garlic granules
- 1 tsp onion powder
- ½ tsp dried chilli flakes (or more to taste)
- 1 tsp smoked paprika
- ½ tsp Chinese five-spice (optional, adds depth)
- 1 tsp sea salt
- ½ tsp freshly ground black pepper
- 2 spring onions, finely sliced
- 1 small red chilli, thinly sliced (optional, to garnish)
- Small handful of fresh coriander, chopped (optional)
- Lime juice or dipping sauce, to serve

These wedges have been a staple on my barbecue for years, whether it's using leftover baked potatoes or cooking from scratch, they never last long. Tossed in a punchy salt and chilli seasoning and cooked over coals until golden and crispy, they're a guaranteed crowd-pleaser. The smokiness from the barbecue adds something special that you just can't replicate in the oven.

Serve them as a banging side with grilled meats, tuck them into wraps or top them with cheese and hot sauce for an easy snack platter. Either way, they'll steal the show.

Prep

Scrub the raw potatoes (no need to peel), then cut them into chunky wedges. Parboil in salted water for 6–7 minutes until just tender, then drain well and let them steam-dry. This helps them crisp up beautifully. If using leftover baked potatoes, cut into wedges.

Toss the wedges in a bowl with the oil, garlic granules, onion powder, chilli flakes, smoked paprika, five-spice (if using), salt and pepper. Make sure they're well coated.

Set your barbecue for indirect cooking at around 200–220°C (400–425°F).

Grill

Place the wedges on a tray or in a cast-iron skillet and cook indirectly on the barbecue with the lid closed for 20–30 minutes. Turn occasionally to ensure even colouring.

Once the wedges are nearly done – golden and crisp – move them to the direct side of the grill for a final blast of heat to add a bit of char.

Serve

Toss the hot wedges with sliced spring onions and chilli, if using, then scatter over some chopped coriander if you're feeling fancy. Serve them hot with a squeeze of lime or your favourite dipping sauce.

→ **Hint of Heat:** Try tossing them in gochugaru chilli flakes or Sichuan pepper for a different twist.

→ **Load Them Up:** Add grated cheese and pop back on the barbecue with the lid closed for loaded wedges.

→ **Chill Out:** Serve with soured cream and sweet chilli for a cooling contrast.

GRILLED ELOTE STREET CORN

Fire-kissed corn slathered in lime-chilli crema, showered with cheese

Prep Time: 10 minutes

Cook Time: 10 minutes

SERVES 4–6

- 4–6 corn cobs, husks removed
- 2 tbsp avocado oil or olive oil
- 90g (3½oz) soured cream
- 2 tbsp mayonnaise
- Zest and juice of 1 lime
- 1 small garlic clove, finely grated
- 1 small avocado, mashed
- 1 tbsp feta, crumbled
- 1 tsp chilli powder (or Tajín for a citrusy kick)
- Fresh coriander, chopped
- Extra lime wedges, to serve

No taco night is complete without elote – Mexican street corn that's smoky, spicy and absolutely addictive. I first tried it from a food truck in San Francisco, slathered in crema, lime and chilli, and it was love at first bite. This version adds avocado and fresh herbs for that freshness, but still keeps the messy, delicious spirit of the original.

Prep
Preheat the grill to medium-high. Brush the corn with the oil.

In a small bowl, whisk together the soured cream, mayo, lime zest and juice, garlic and the mashed avocado.

Grill
Grill the corn, turning occasionally, until nicely charred and tender, about 10 minutes in total.

When the corn comes off the grill, slather each ear generously with the crema mixture.

Serve
Sprinkle with the feta, a pinch of chilli powder or Tajín, and some chopped coriander.

Serve immediately with extra lime wedges for squeezing.

→ **Make It A Salad:** Slice the kernels off the corn cobs after grilling and mix with the crema, cheese, herbs and spices – perfect for a taco bar side dish.

→ **Spice It Up:** Add chopped jalapeños or a drizzle of hot sauce to the crema.

MEXICO-INSPIRED HALLOUMI TACOS

Crispy-edged halloumi tucked into warm tortillas with a chilli-lime kick

Prep Time: 20 minutes
Cook Time: 15 minutes

SERVES 4

FOR THE RUB
- 2 tsp smoked paprika
- 2 tsp brown sugar
- 2 tsp dried oregano
- 1 tsp cumin seeds
- 1 tsp dried chilli flakes
- Zest of 1 lime
- Sea salt and freshly ground black pepper

FOR THE TACOS
- 250g (9oz) halloumi, cut into slices
- 2 tbsp rapeseed oil or olive oil
- 2 corn cobs, husks removed
- 8 small soft corn tortillas (or flour tortillas for a softer bite)
- 1 ripe avocado, sliced
- ½ red onion, thinly sliced
- 1 small chilli, thinly sliced (optional)
- Handful of fresh coriander leaves
- 110g (4oz) soured cream
- Lime wedges, for squeezing and to serve

Inspired by the vibrant flavours and grilling techniques of Mexico, these grilled halloumi tacos combine the savoury richness of the cheese with a spicy rub, fresh ingredients and classic Mexican garnishes. The smoky, tangy and slightly sweet rub paired with the crisp, grilled cheese creates a delicious taco experience that transports you straight to a Mexican beachside fiesta.

Prep
In a small bowl, mix together the smoked paprika, brown sugar, oregano, cumin seeds, chilli flakes and lime zest. Season generously with salt and pepper to combine.

Drizzle the halloumi slices with the oil and then sprinkle the rub evenly over both sides of the cheese, pressing it in so that it sticks.

Heat the grill to medium-high heat (180–230°C/350–450°F).

Grill
Place the corn ears directly on the grill and cook for about 8 minutes, turning occasionally, until the corn is tender and has nice grill marks. Once cooked, remove from the grill and set aside to cool slightly. Once cool enough to handle, cut the corn kernels off the cob and set aside.

Place the halloumi slices on the grill over a high heat. Grill for about 2 minutes per side, or until the halloumi is golden brown and crispy on the outside but still soft and warm on the inside.

While the halloumi is grilling, heat the tortillas on the grill for about 15–20 seconds per side, until warm and lightly charred.

Serve
Place the warm tortillas on a serving platter. For each taco, top with a few slices of grilled halloumi. Add a handful of the grilled corn kernels, then load up with avocado slices, red onion, sliced chilli and fresh coriander leaves. Drizzle with soured cream and squeeze fresh lime juice over the top.

Serve immediately with extra lime wedges on the side for a burst of freshness.

BBQ ROASTED VEGETABLES

Fire-kissed with a zesty dressing

Prep Time: 15 minutes

Cook Time: 35–40 minutes

SERVES 4

- 3 red onions, quartered
- 3 potatoes, scrubbed and cut into wedges
- 2 aubergines, thickly sliced
- 2 yellow peppers, deseeded and thickly sliced
- 4 tomatoes, halved
- 2 tbsp olive oil
- Sea salt and freshly ground black pepper
- Parmesan shavings, to serve

FOR THE DRESSING

- 3 tbsp extra virgin olive oil
- 2 tbsp honey
- 1 tbsp balsamic vinegar
- Finely grated zest and juice of ½ lemon

Charred, tender and full of flavour – these barbecue-roasted vegetables are the perfect balance of sweet, smoky and sharp. Tossed in a bright, honey-lemon balsamic dressing and finished with Parmesan shavings, this dish works brilliantly as a side or a veggie main. Ideal alongside grilled meats or served warm with crusty bread, this is simple barbecue food elevated by the flame.

Prep

Set your barbecue for direct medium-high heat (180–230°C/ 350–450°F). Use a covered grill if possible, to create an oven-like environment.

Place all the chopped vegetables in a shallow roasting tin or barbecue-safe tray. Drizzle with the olive oil, season with salt and pepper, and toss to coat evenly. Spread them out in a single layer.

In a small bowl or jar, mix the olive oil, honey, balsamic vinegar and lemon zest and juice until well combined.

Grill

Place the tray directly on the barbecue grates. Cover with the lid and cook for 35–40 minutes, stirring once or twice, until the vegetables are soft, caramelised and slightly charred at the edges.

Serve

Once the vegetables are cooked, drizzle over the dressing and toss gently to coat. Divide between serving plates and top with Parmesan shavings.

→ **Add Protein:** Serve with grilled halloumi, chicken thighs or lamb chops to make it a full meal.
→ **Boost the Base:** Add cooked grains like couscous or bulgur for a warm barbecue salad.
→ **Spice It Up:** Add a pinch of smoked paprika, cumin or chilli flakes to the dressing.
→ **Add Crunch:** Scatter toasted pine nuts or pumpkin seeds over the finished dish.

HEIRLOOM TOMATO & ROASTED GARLIC GALETTE

A rustic late-summer showstopper

Prep Time: 15 minutes

Cook Time: 20–25 minutes

SERVES 4

- 2 sheets of ready-rolled puff pastry
- 10 mixed heirloom tomatoes, sliced into thick rounds
- 10 heirloom cherry tomatoes, cut in half (or leave some whole for a juicy pop)
- 6 tbsp chopped roasted garlic (see page 242)
- 1 tbsp finely chopped jamón ibérico (optional, for that umami boost)
- A few sprigs of fresh thyme or Spanish oregano
- 1 egg, beaten
- Coarse sea salt, for sprinkling
- Spanish extra virgin olive oil, for drizzling

Buttery, flaky pastry loaded with jammy heirloom tomatoes and sweet roasted garlic – this sun-drenched galette brings together the rustic beauty of the French countryside with the bold flavours of Spain. Think of it as tapas with a bit of a French soul, perfect for long afternoons. Inspired by a stopover in San Sebastián many years ago, where the tomatoes were so ripe they tasted like summer itself, this dish pairs the richness of slow-roasted garlic with the brightness of heirloom tomatoes. A little jamón for depth, a drizzle of Spanish olive oil for flair, and you've got a golden pastry that looks like a painting and eats like a dream. If you can, get hold of deep red, golden yellow and striped green tomatoes.

Prep

Preheat the barbecue or oven to 220°C/200°C fan (425°F). Line a baking sheet with baking parchment.

Roll out the puff pastry onto the baking sheet. Score a 5mm (¼in) border around the edge with a sharp knife, being careful not to cut through.

Arrange the tomatoes inside the border, mixing sizes and colours for visual flair.

Scatter the roasted garlic across the top, along with the jamón bits, if using. Tuck a few thyme sprigs between the tomatoes.

Brush the pastry border with the beaten egg.

Grill

Bake on the barbecue or in the oven for 20–25 minutes, or until the crust is golden and puffed and the tomatoes are bubbling gently. Remove from the barbecue or oven.

Serve

Finish with a sprinkle of sea salt and a generous drizzle of good olive oil. Serve warm or at room temperature.

➜ **Creamy Kick:** Add whipped goat's cheese or ricotta under the tomatoes for an extra creamy layer.

➜ **Veggie Alternative:** Swap jamón for caramelised shallots to keep it veggie but still full of depth.

➜ **Make It Mini:** Turn it into bite-sized tartlets using a muffin tin and smaller rounds of pastry.

ZESTY MANGO, HALLOUMI & BLACK BEAN SALAD

A BBQ-ready salad bursting with colour

Prep Time: 20 minutes

Cook Time: 5-7 minutes

SERVES 6 AS A SIDE OR 4 AS A MAIN

- 400g (14oz) tin of black beans, drained and rinsed
- 2 large handfuls of baby spinach
- 500g (17oz) heritage tomatoes, chopped into large chunks
- ½ cucumber, halved, deseeded and sliced on the diagonal
- 1 ripe mango, peeled and chopped into chunks
- 1 large red onion, halved and finely sliced
- 6-8 radishes, thinly sliced
- 250g (9oz) halloumi, sliced into batons or slabs
- Olive oil, for brushing
- 2 avocados, sliced
- 100g (3½oz) feta, crumbled
- Small handful of fresh herbs (from dressing)

FOR THE HERB DRESSING

- Small bunch of fresh mint
- Small bunch of fresh coriander
- Small bunch of fresh basil
- 1 fat green chilli, deseeded and roughly chopped
- 1 garlic clove
- Zest and juice of 2 limes
- 2 tbsp white wine vinegar
- 2 tsp honey
- 100ml (3½fl oz) extra virgin olive oil
- Pinch each of sea salt and freshly ground black pepper

This salad was made for outdoor eating, with its big flavours, fresh textures and a punchy green herb dressing that brings everything to life. Golden-seared halloumi, sweet mango, creamy avocado and a heap of vibrant veg. It's fresh but filling, and a serious looker when laid out on the table. A real crowd-pleaser.

Prep

First make the herb dressing. Reserve some of the herbs for the salad. Blitz the remaining herbs, green chilli, garlic, lime zest and juice, vinegar, honey and oil in a food processor until smooth and vibrant. Taste and season with salt and pepper. Chill until needed. It'll keep for a day in the fridge and gets even better as the flavours mingle.

Spread the black beans and spinach across a large serving board or platter. Arrange the tomatoes, cucumber, mango, onion and radishes over the top. Use your hands to gently mix and toss the ingredients, keeping the salad loose and rustic.

Grill

Brush the halloumi slices with a little olive oil and grill over direct medium-high heat (180-230°C/ 350-450°F) for 2-3 minutes per side until golden and lightly charred. You want crisp edges and a soft, gooey middle. Set aside to cool slightly before adding to the salad.

Serve

Add the avocado slices, crumbled feta and grilled halloumi pieces to the rest of the salad. Scatter over the reserved fresh herbs and serve with a jug of that zingy green herb dressing on the side. It's perfect warm or chilled, as a vibrant side or a showstopping main.

BBQ PORTOBELLO MUSHROOM BURGERS *with* SMOKED CHEDDAR & CHIPOTLE MAYO

Big flavour, no meat required

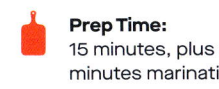

Prep Time:
15 minutes, plus 30 minutes marinating

Cook Time:
25–30 minutes

SERVES 4

| 3 tbsp balsamic vinegar |
| 2 tbsp soy sauce |
| 2 tbsp olive oil |
| 2 garlic cloves, finely grated |
| 1 tsp smoked paprika |
| Pinch of freshly ground black pepper |
| 4 large Portobello mushrooms, stalks trimmed |

FOR THE CHIPOTLE MAYO

| 4 tbsp mayonnaise |
| 1–2 tsp chipotle paste (adjust to taste) |
| Squeeze of lime juice |

FOR THE CARAMELISED ONIONS

| 1 tbsp butter |
| 2 large red onions, thinly sliced |
| 1 tsp brown sugar |
| 1 tsp balsamic vinegar |
| Salt, to taste |

TO FORM THE BURGERS

| 4 slices of smoked Cheddar |
| 4 brioche buns, halved and lightly toasted |
| Handful of rocket or baby spinach |
| Pickled jalapeños (optional) |

If you're after a veggie burger that's anything but an afterthought, this one's for you. These Portobello mushrooms soak up a punchy marinade of garlic with balsamic vinegar and soy sauce, then hit the grill for that smoky charred edge that gives them serious main-character energy. Layer them up with gooey smoked Cheddar, sweet caramelised onions and a generous dollop of chipotle mayo in a toasted brioche bun – trust me, no one's going to miss the meat.

Prep

In a bowl, whisk together the balsamic vinegar, soy sauce, olive oil, garlic, smoked paprika and black pepper. Add the mushrooms and toss to coat. Let them marinate for at least 30 minutes, turning occasionally to soak up all that bold flavour.

Mix the mayo, chipotle paste and lime juice in a small bowl. Adjust the heat and tang to your liking.

Fire up your barbecue for medium-high direct heat (180–230°C/350–450°F).

Grill

In a skillet or cast-iron pan over the hob or BBQ, melt the butter over a medium-low heat. Add the onions and cook gently for 15–20 minutes, stirring now and again until they're soft, sweet and golden. Stir in the brown sugar and a splash of balsamic vinegar, then cook for another couple of minutes to glaze. Season with a pinch of salt and set aside.

Place the marinated mushrooms on the barbecue, gill-side down, and grill for 4–5 minutes per side, or until tender and nicely charred. In the last couple of minutes, flip and top each one with a slice of smoked Cheddar so it melts over the top.

Serve

Toast your buns on the grill, cut-side down, until golden. Spread the chipotle mayo on both the top and bottom buns. Stack the grilled mushrooms onto the bases, top with caramelised onions, a handful of rocket and a few jalapeños if you fancy some heat. Crown with the top bun and serve straight off the board.

BBQ-SEARED LEEK BARRELS *with* SMOKY ROMESCO SAUCE

Charred, sweet leeks with a bold Spanish-inspired kick

Prep Time: 20 minutes, plus 15 minutes chilling

Cook Time: 10–12 minutes

SERVES 4

- 4 large leeks, trimmed and cut into 5–8cm (2–3in) barrels
- Olive oil, for brushing
- Sea salt, to taste

FOR THE SMOKY ROMESCO SAUCE

- 40g (1½oz) almonds
- 2 roasted red peppers (jarred or home-roasted)
- 2 ripe roasted tomatoes
- 1–2 garlic cloves
- 1 tbsp sherry vinegar, or red wine vinegar
- 1 tsp smoked paprika
- Pinch of cayenne pepper (optional, for heat)
- 60–120ml (2½–4fl oz) extra virgin olive oil

This one's proof that veg can be the star of the show. Thick-cut leeks are grilled over flames until golden and blistered, then served up with a smoky romesco sauce that brings richness, heat and just the right amount of tang. It's simple but full of big flavours – ideal for a barbecue spread where you want to impress without overcomplicating things. Whether you're serving it with crusty bread as a main or alongside your grilled meats, this one holds its own.

Prep

Toast your almonds in a dry pan until golden and fragrant. Add them to a blender with the roasted peppers, tomatoes, garlic, vinegar, smoked paprika and cayenne. Blitz until mostly smooth, then slowly drizzle in the olive oil while blending to get your desired consistency. Season with salt, then chill for at least 15 minutes to allow the flavours to deepen.

Grill

Toss the leek barrels with olive oil and a pinch of salt, making sure they're well coated. Grill over direct medium heat (180–230°C/350–450°F), turning occasionally, until they're charred on the outside and soft right through – 10–12 minutes depending on thickness. You want good grill marks and a little caramelisation.

Serve

Pile the seared leeks onto a platter and spoon over that smoky romesco. Serve warm with crusty bread for scooping, or alongside grilled chicken, steak or halloumi.

GARAM MASALA CAULIFLOWER STEAKS *with* MINT CHUTNEY & PICKLED ONIONS

Fire-grilled veggie feasting at its finest

Prep Time: 20 minutes, plus 1 hour or overnight marinating

Cook Time: 20–25 minutes

SERVES 4

- 2 large cauliflowers, leaves removed
- 200ml (7fl oz) natural yoghurt or dairy-free alternative
- 1 tbsp lemon juice
- 3 garlic cloves, finely grated
- 2.5cm (1in) piece of fresh ginger, finely grated
- 2 tsp ground cumin
- 2 tsp smoked paprika
- 1 tsp ground turmeric
- 1½ tsp garam masala
- 1 tsp ground coriander
- ½ tsp cayenne pepper
- Sea salt and freshly ground black pepper
- Olive oil, for brushing

FOR THE MINT DRIZZLE

- Large handful of fresh mint leaves
- Small bunch of fresh coriander
- 1 green chilli, deseeded
- Juice of 1 lime
- 2 tbsp yoghurt

FOR THE PICKLED ONIONS

- 1 red onion, thinly sliced
- 3 tbsp white wine vinegar
- 1 tsp sugar

TO SERVE

- Warm naan or flatbreads
- Fresh coriander
- Extra lime wedges

Fire-grilled veggie feasting at its finest. When you're feeding a crowd and want to bring something bold and meat-free to the barbecue, these cauliflower steaks deliver in spades. Inspired by the punchy flavours of Indian tandoori cooking, but cooked over open flame, they're smoky, spicy and beautifully charred on the outside while staying tender in the middle. I first threw these together on a whim at a summer barbecue and watched a table of meat-eaters go absolutely silent with the first bite – always a good sign! Serve them up with a zingy mint chutney, a pile of tangy pickled onions and warm naan to mop it all up. It's a proper veggie centrepiece that brings the heat.

Prep

Slice each cauliflower from top to bottom into 2–3 thick steaks (about 3cm/1¼in thick), keeping the core intact where possible to hold them together. Save any florets that fall off for grilling too.

For the marinade, whisk together the yoghurt, lemon juice, garlic, ginger and all the spices in a large bowl. Season well with salt and pepper. Brush or spoon the marinade generously over both sides of each cauliflower steak. Place on a tray, cover, and marinate in the fridge for at least 1 hour (or up to overnight).

In a food processor or blender, combine all the mint drizzle ingredients and blitz until smooth. Adjust the flavour with lime juice and salt to taste.

Combine the sliced onion with vinegar, sugar and a pinch of salt in a bowl. Leave to sit and pickle while you finish the rest of the dish – 10–15 minutes is plenty.

Set your grill up for medium-high direct heat (180–230°C/350–450°F). Oil the grates well to prevent sticking.

Grill

Place the steaks directly over the heat. Grill for 5–6 minutes on each side until deeply charred and fork-tender. Brush with a little oil as they cook and move to indirect heat if they start to catch too quickly.

Serve

Lay the grilled cauliflower steaks on a platter. Spoon over the mint drizzle, scatter with the pickled onions, and serve with warm naan on the side. Finish with fresh coriander and extra lime wedges for squeezing.

PORK
ORK
PORK
POR
Pork

Pork

PORK

ORK

Pork

ORK

STICKY PORK BELLY BURNT ENDS *with* SWEET CIDER GLAZE

Smoked, soft pork-belly cubes – sticky, glossy and downright addictive

Prep Time: 30 minutes

Cook Time: 5–6 hours

SERVES 6–8

- 2.3kg (5lb) pork belly, skin removed
- 120g (4oz) pork rub (use your house blend or SPG with paprika and brown sugar)
- Apple cider vinegar, for spritzing

FOR THE GLAZE
- 325g (11oz) honey
- 110g (4oz) light brown sugar
- 120ml (4fl oz) BBQ sauce (your favourite sweet-style works great, or try my Apple & Irish Whiskey Sauce, page 231)
- 6 tbsp unsalted butter, cut into cubes

There's something undeniably magic about pork belly burnt ends. It's one of those cuts that turns from humble to heavenly with a bit of time and fire. This version brings together everything I love in a bite – sweet, sticky, smoky, with buttery-soft pork and a crackle of bark on every edge. Perfect for nachos, topping a burger, served with mac and cheese or just enjoyed by themselves as some beer nibbles with friends. These burnt ends are the kind of thing that people remember long after the grill's gone cold. Fork optional. Napkins required.

Prep
Trim your pork belly into 3–4cm (1¼–1½in) cubes. Aim for even sizing so they cook at the same rate. Season generously on all sides with your pork rub. Let them sit at room temperature while you fire up the smoker.

Set up your smoker or barbecue for indirect heat at 120°C (250°F), using cherry or apple wood for a sweet-smoke flavour.

In a bowl, whisk together the honey, brown sugar and BBQ sauce until smooth and combined.

Grill
Place the pork cubes on a wire rack or directly on the grates if you've got the space, just make sure they're not touching. Smoke for 3½–4 hours, spritzing with apple cider vinegar every hour to keep them juicy and help the bark set.

Once the pork has taken on a deep, mahogany colour and the fat is starting to render, transfer the cubes to a deep foil tray or ovenproof dish. Pour the glaze over the pork and toss to coat well. Dot the butter over the top, then cover tightly with foil.

Return to the smoker and cook for another 1½–2 hours until the pork hits 90–95°C (194–203°F internal temperature). The burnt ends should feel pillowy-soft and tender when pressed, like the barbecue version of a marshmallow.

Serve
Let them rest for 10–15 minutes, uncovered. Toss once more in the glaze before serving. They're sticky, juicy and wildly addictive.

➔ **Bourbon Glaze:** Add a splash of bourbon to the glaze for a boozy caramel twist.
➔ **Spicy Kick:** Stir in a teaspoon of hot sauce or chilli jam.
➔ **Taco-Ready:** Shred the ends and serve in soft tortillas with pickled red onion and slaw.

SMOKY BACON, POTATO & CORN CHOWDER

Silky rich soup – comfort by the spoonful

Prep Time: 15 minutes

Cook Time: 25–30 minutes

SERVES 4

- 3 tbsp oil or butter (or use bacon fat for extra flavour)
- 225g (8oz) chopped bacon
- 1 large onion, finely diced
- 2 carrots, diced
- 2 celery sticks, diced
- 2 garlic cloves, minced
- 1 tsp chopped fresh thyme
- 30g (1oz) plain flour
- 500ml (17fl oz) chicken broth
- 480ml (16fl oz) whole milk or double cream
- 675g (1½lb) potatoes, diced into small cubes (peeled if you prefer)
- 175g (6oz) sweetcorn (fresh, tinned or frozen)
- Sea salt and freshly ground black pepper

TO SERVE (optional)

- 4 rashers of streaky bacon, cooked and crumbled
- Chopped chives or spring onions
- Sourdough or crusty bread

This one's born from a misty morning in the Mourne Mountains – where the air's crisp and the views are unreal. It was one of those slow, foggy starts on the Northern Irish coast, where lighting the barbecue, for me, felt more like a necessity than a luxury. I threw together what was left in the cooler – a bit of bacon, some tinned corn and a few spuds – and ended up with a chowder that's stuck with me ever since. It's rich, comforting and packs just enough smoke to warm the bones. A proper fireside bowl for wet weekends and campsite cook-ups.

Prep

Heat the oil, butter or bacon fat in a large pan over a medium heat with the chopped bacon. When browned, remove the bacon. Toss in the onion, carrots and celery, and let them soften slowly in the remaining fat for around 8–10 minutes. You're aiming for tender, not browned.

Add the garlic and thyme to the softened veg and cook for another minute, just until aromatic. Stir through the flour and cook for 2–3 minutes, stirring constantly – this gives the soup body.

Slowly pour in your broth, scraping the bottom to lift up all that flavour. Follow with the milk or cream, then stir in the diced potatoes. Bring to a gentle boil, then reduce heat and simmer until the spuds are fork-tender – about 12 minutes.

Stir in the chopped bacon and corn, letting everything heat through for another 5 minutes. Taste and season generously with salt and pepper.

Serve

Ladle the chowder into bowls and top with crispy bacon bits and chopped chives or spring onions, if you fancy. Serve with a warm chunk of sourdough or crusty bread to mop up every last spoonful.

➜ **Vegetarian Version:** Swap bacon for smoked Cheddar, or use roasted mushrooms for a deep umami punch.

➜ **Make It Heartier:** Stir through leftover pulled pork or shredded BBQ chicken for a meatier chowder.

SPICY PORK CHOPS with MANGO SALSA

Some sweet heat, island-style

Prep Time: 15 minutes, plus 6–24 hours marinating

Cook Time: 20 minutes

SERVES 4

- 4 habanero or Scotch bonnet chillies
- 5cm (2in) piece of fresh ginger, peeled and roughly chopped
- 4 garlic cloves, smashed
- 1 tbsp ground cinnamon
- 1 tbsp ground allspice
- 1 tbsp ground nutmeg
- 3 tbsp molasses
- Good pinch of sea salt
- 4 bone-in pork chops
- Oil, for greasing

FOR THE MANGO SALSA

- 1 large ripe mango, peeled, stoned and diced
- 1 shallot, finely minced
- 1 jalapeño, finely diced
- Small bunch of fresh coriander leaves, chopped
- Zest and juice of 1 lime
- 2 tbsp olive oil

This one takes me straight back to the laidback rhythm of island life, somewhere warm, with steel drums in the background and the scent of spices drifting over from the grill. We first grilled pork this way after coming back from a trip to the Caribbean, trying to recreate that bold, fire-kissed flavour with what we had at home, and I think we did it justice.

The marinade is fiery and rich, with Scotch bonnets, warm spices and molasses to give it depth and sweetness. It's a full-flavour experience, mellowed out by a cooling mango salsa. When the pork hits the grill, you know something good is coming – that smoky, spicy aroma is impossible to ignore. Pair with an ice-cold Red Stripe or a spiced rum punch, maybe even add some grilled pineapple or a splash of jerk sauce on the side for extra flair and a feast that'll transport you straight to the tropics.

Prep

In a blender, combine the chillies, ginger, garlic, cinnamon, allspice, nutmeg, molasses and salt. Blitz to a coarse purée.

Place the pork chops in a ceramic dish and coat with the marinade. Cover and refrigerate for 6–24 hours.

Make the salsa. In a bowl, toss together the mango, shallot, jalapeño, coriander, lime zest and juice and olive oil. Cover and refrigerate until ready to serve.

Preheat the grill to medium-high (180–230°C/350–450°F) and brush the grate with oil.

Grill

Grill the pork chops for 6 minutes per side, then reduce the heat or move to indirect heat. Cook for another 6–8 minutes until the internal temperature hits 60°C (140°F) and the meat is just slightly pink in the centre.

Transfer to a plate, cover with foil, and rest for 10 minutes. The temperature of the chops will continue to rise another 3–5°C (37–41°F) during the rest period.

Serve

Plate the pork chops with the mango salsa. A scoop of white rice or coconut rice on the side rounds it out perfectly.

COLA-GLAZED HAM *with* BLACK PEPPER & MARMALADE GLAZE & PROPER YORKSHIRE PUDS

A sweet, smoky roast ham finished over fire and served with golden-crisp Yorkshires

Prep Time: 30 minutes, plus 1 hour or overnight soaking

Cook Time: 2½–3 hours

SERVES 6–8

FOR THE HAM

- 2kg (4½lb) unsmoked gammon joint, skin on
- 6 litres (10½ pints) Coca-Cola (or enough to submerge the ham)
- 1 large orange, sliced
- 2 tsp whole cloves, plus a handful for studding
- 1 tbsp black peppercorns
- 1 jar good-quality marmalade
- Splash of orange juice, for basting (optional)
- Sea salt and freshly ground black pepper

FOR THE YORKSHIRE PUDDINGS

- 200ml (7fl oz) whole milk
- 4 large eggs
- 200g (7oz) plain flour
- Pinch of sea salt
- Rapeseed or sunflower oil, for cooking

This one's a firm festive favourite, but one we also cook at several times throughout the year. It's part retro, part rockstar – the ham is poached in full-fat Coca-Cola for that deep, sticky-sweet flavour, then blasted on the barbecue or in the oven with a fiery glaze of black pepper and orange marmalade. Serve it alongside Yorkshire puddings because, yes, they belong with ham too. Especially if you've got that marmalade baste to mop up.

Prep

Soak the gammon in cold water for a few hours, changing the water once or twice. This helps draw out excess salt from the cure.

For the Yorkshire puddings, whisk the milk and eggs in a jug, then gradually add the flour and salt. Mix until smooth and lump-free, then refrigerate for at least 1 hour (overnight is even better).

Place the gammon in a large stockpot and pour in enough Coca-Cola to cover it fully. Add the orange slices, cloves and peppercorns. Bring to a gentle simmer and cook for 1–1½ hours, depending on the size of your joint. The meat should feel tender but not falling apart.

Once poached, remove the gammon and let it cool slightly. Carefully peel off the skin, leaving a good layer of fat. Score the fat into diamonds and stud each cross-section with a clove. Sprinkle generously with black pepper.

Preheat your barbecue (indirect) or oven to 180°C (350°F).

Grill

Place the ham into a roasting tray and roast, uncovered, for 10 minutes to begin crisping the fat. Then spoon over the marmalade – it'll melt and caramelise beautifully. Return to the barbecue and roast for 45–60 minutes, basting every 10 minutes with the juices. If things start to look too dry, splash in a little orange juice to keep the glaze silky. Once cooked, let the ham rest for 10–15 minutes before slicing.

Once the ham is done, raise the temperature of your barbecue (or oven) to 250°C (475°F) and add a teaspoon of oil into the holes of a muffin tin. Heat until the oil is smoking hot.

Working quickly, pour the cold batter evenly into the hot oil. Shut the barbecue lid (or oven door) and don't open it – not even for a peek – for 25–30 minutes until puffed and golden.

Serve
Serve thick slices of ham with the bubbling glaze spooned over and Yorkshire puddings on the side to mop up all that sticky goodness.

→ **Festive Flair:** Add star anise or cinnamon sticks to the poaching liquid for an aromatic twist.

→ **No Waste:** Use in toasted sandwiches with mature Cheddar, pickled onions and mustard mayo.

PULLED PORK with CIDER MOP & TANGY SLAW

Low, slow and made to share

 Prep Time: 20 minutes, plus marinating overnight (optional)

 Cook Time: 6–8 hours

 Feeds a Crowd

SERVES 8–10

- 2.5–3kg (5½–6½lb) pork shoulder, bone-in, skin removed
- 3 tbsp yellow mustard
- 3 tbsp BBQ rub (see below or use your favourite blend)
- 240ml (8fl oz) apple juice or cider

FOR THE BBQ BUTT RUB

- 2 tbsp sea salt
- 2 tbsp soft brown sugar
- 1 tbsp smoked paprika
- 1 tbsp garlic granules
- 1 tbsp onion powder
- 1 tsp cayenne pepper
- 1 tsp ground cumin
- 1 tsp freshly ground black pepper

FOR THE CIDER MOP SAUCE (optional)

- 240ml (8fl oz) Magners Irish Cider
- 120ml (4fl oz) apple cider vinegar
- 2 tbsp brown sugar
- 1 tsp dried chilli flakes
- 1 tsp Dijon mustard

TO SERVE

- Soft brioche rolls, toasted, or flatbreads
- Tangy slaw (red cabbage, carrot and apple tossed with cider vinegar and a pinch of sugar, or see page 245)
- BBQ sauce or cider vinegar

There's something about pulled pork that just hits all the right notes – smoky, juicy, sweet and savoury all in one bite. This recipe was inspired by my trips to the US, where the smell of smoke often hits you before you've even got out of the car. The pitmaster mopped the pork with apple cider vinegar and served it on a soft bun with a crunchy slaw. Back home, I gave it a few tweaks with Irish cider, a bold rub and that signature Onlyslaggin' BBQ style.

Prep

Start by trimming any excess fat from the pork shoulder. Slather it all over with yellow mustard, it helps the rub stick and adds a subtle tang.

Mix the rub ingredients in a bowl and massage generously into the pork. Wrap tightly in cling film and chill overnight, if you've got the time.

Combine all the cider mop sauce ingredients, if using.

Preheat your smoker or barbecue to 120–135°C (250–275°F) using a mix of charcoal and fruit wood like apple or cherry for a mild sweetness. If you're using a water pan, add a splash of cider or apple juice or maybe some herbs for extra aroma. Set up for indirect cooking.

Grill

Place the pork shoulder directly on the grill or on a rack above the water pan. Cook with the lid down for 6–8 hours, depending on size, until the internal temperature hits 92–95°C (198–203°F) and the meat feels soft and pulls apart easily.

Spritz with apple juice or cider every hour or so after the first 2 hours to keep the bark from drying out. Or mop with the cider mop every 45 minutes for a bit more tang.

Once cooked, remove the pork and wrap it in foil. Let it rest for at least 30–45 minutes. This step is crucial as resting helps all those juices settle back into the meat.

Serve

Using two forks or your hands (gloves help if it's hot), shred the pork into strands, discarding any large fatty bits. Mix with any collected juices or a splash of mop sauce for moisture.

Pile the pork high onto toasted rolls or flatbreads. Top with a crunchy slaw and drizzle over your favourite BBQ sauce or some extra cider vinegar.

→ `Deep Sauce:` Add a splash of bourbon to your mop sauce for deeper flavour.
→ `Waste Not:` Use leftover pulled pork in mac and cheese, loaded fries or stuffed peppers. Or make tacos with lime crema and pickled onions.

MOJO-STYLE PORK ROAST

Citrus, smoke and serious flavour

 Prep Time: 20 minutes, plus overnight marinating

 Cook Time: Approx. 1½–2 hours (varies by roast size)

SERVES 6–8

- 175ml (6fl oz) olive oil
- 1 tbsp orange zest
- 175ml (6fl oz) fresh orange juice
- ½ tbsp lime zest
- 60ml (2½fl oz) fresh lime juice
- 30g (1oz) fresh coriander, finely chopped
- 1 tbsp finely chopped fresh mint leaves
- 8 garlic cloves, minced
- 2 tsp dried oregano
- 2 tsp ground cumin
- 1 tbsp brown sugar
- 1.1kg (2½lb) boneless pork roast, fat trimmed closely
- 1 tsp salt
- 1 tsp black pepper

This Cuban-inspired pork roast is all about bright citrus, bold herbs and deep flavour. A 24-hour marinade of orange, lime, coriander, mint, garlic and spices transforms a humble pork roast into a juicy, tender centrepiece. Cooked low and slow over indirect barbecue heat, it's ideal sliced up in tacos and sandwiches, or served simply with rice and beans.

Prep

In a large bowl or resealable bag, combine the olive oil, orange zest and juice, lime zest and juice, coriander, mint, garlic, oregano, cumin and brown sugar until well combined.

Place the pork roast into the marinade, turning to ensure it's fully coated. Cover or seal and refrigerate overnight.

Remove the pork from the marinade and pat it dry. Season all over with salt and pepper.

Set up your barbecue for indirect cooking at 200°C (400°F).

Grill

Place the pork over indirect heat and cook with the lid closed until the internal temperature reaches 61°C (142°F). Cooking time will depend on the size and thickness of the roast, but it is typically 1½–2 hours.

Serve

Remove from the barbecue and rest the pork, loosely covered with foil, for 15–20 minutes (roughly a quarter of the total cooking time). Slice and serve.

→ **Make It A Feast:** Serve in soft rolls with pickles and mustard for a Cuban-style sandwich.

→ **Add Sides:** Try with black beans and rice, grilled corn cobs or a citrus-dressed slaw.

→ **Batch Cook:** Double the marinade and use it on chicken thighs or pork chops later in the week.

→ **Smoke Boost:** Add a small chunk of citrus or pecan wood for a subtle, sweet smoke layer.

→ **No Waste:** Leftovers make epic tacos, quesadillas or breakfast hash.

IRISH-STYLE PORCHETTA *with* CIDER, APPLE & MUSTARD CRUST

Sunday roast meets smokehouse

Prep Time: 30 minutes, plus 1 hour marinating

Cook Time: 2½–3 hours

Equipment: Butcher's string, for tying

Feeds a Crowd

SERVES 12–16

- 3.5–4kg (8–8.8lb) pork belly, skin on (approx. 40 × 25cm/16 × 10in, 4cm/1½in thick)
- 3 tbsp wholegrain mustard
- 2 apples, grated (Bramley or Pink Lady work well)
- 1 tbsp cider vinegar
- 3 tbsp fresh sage, finely chopped
- 1 tbsp fresh rosemary, finely chopped
- 1 tbsp fresh thyme leaves
- 4 garlic cloves, minced
- 1 tsp freshly ground black pepper
- 2 tsp sea salt
- 1 tsp ground allspice (optional, adds warmth)
- 2–3kg (4½–6½lb) boneless pork loin (same length as belly)
- 2 tsp fine salt

There's something timeless about gathering folk around the fire for a proper feast – and nowhere does that better than the Irish countryside. This porchetta is my nod to both Italian tradition and Irish ingredients, inspired by slow Sundays in Armagh, where apple orchards reign supreme. This version keeps the belly-wrapped loin technique but swaps out the usual fennel-heavy rub for a mix of tangy mustard, orchard apples, cider vinegar and garden herbs. The crackling stays front and centre, but the flavour leans into a sweet-savoury balance that feels just right for an Irish barbecue spread.

Prep
Pat the pork belly dry and score the skin deeply in a crosshatch pattern. Flip it over and pierce the flesh with a sharp knife – this helps the rub soak in.

In a bowl, mix the mustard, grated apple, cider vinegar, herbs, garlic, pepper, sea salt and allspice, if using. Stir into a thick, textured paste.

Spread the apple-mustard mix evenly over the flesh side of the pork belly. Wrap it tightly in cling film and refrigerate for at least an hour – longer if you have the time. Let it return to room temperature before cooking.

Lay the pork loin along one edge of the belly and roll it up tightly. Tie firmly with butcher's string at 2.5cm (1in) intervals to hold everything together. Rub the skin generously with fine salt.

Fire up your barbecue for indirect cooking at 150°C (302°F). A rotisserie is ideal, but a roasting setup works just as well – make sure to place a drip tray beneath.

Grill
Roast the porchetta for 2½–3 hours, turning occasionally or rotating on the spit, until the skin is blistered and the centre hits 75°C (167°F).

The aroma of cider-soaked pork crackling will let you know you're on the right track.

Serve
Rest under foil for 10–15 minutes. Slice into thick rounds and serve with mustard, apple chutney or alongside some Colcannon.

→ **Smoked Butter Glaze:** For a glossy finish, baste the skin with melted Irish butter mixed with a splash of cider vinegar during the final 30 minutes.

→ **Next-Day Sandwiches:** Stack cold slices in a soft bap with crisp lettuce, mature Cheddar and leftover mustardy juices.

→ **Whiskey Finish:** Add a tablespoon of Irish whiskey to the rub for a warming depth and sweetness.

PORK

2-HOUR BBQ RIBS with APPLE SLAW & CIDER GLAZE

Big-rib flavour on a weeknight clock

Prep Time: 20 minutes, plus 20 minutes resting

Cook Time: 2 hours

Equipment: Apple wood chunks or chips (if using barbecue)

Feeds a Crowd

SERVES 12–16

- 1 rack of pork ribs, membrane removed and excess fat trimmed
- American mustard or olive oil (optional binder)
- BBQ rub of choice (see pages 224–9)
- Magners Irish Cider, for spritzing

FOR THE BBQ SAUCE
- 240ml (8fl oz) Magners Irish Cider
- 75g (3oz) tomato paste
- 60ml (2½fl oz) apple cider vinegar
- 1 tbsp honey
- 2 tbsp low-sodium soy sauce
- ½ tsp chilli powder
- ¼ tsp ground cinnamon
- ¼ tsp black pepper
- Pinch of cayenne pepper

FOR THE SLAW
- 300g (10oz) chopped cabbage
- 1 red apple, cored and chopped
- 1 Granny Smith apple, cored and chopped
- 1 carrot, grated
- 85g (3oz) finely chopped red bell pepper
- 2 green onions, finely chopped
- 75g (3oz) mayonnaise
- 75g (3oz) brown sugar
- 1 tbsp lemon juice

Inspired by harvest season and the iconic Magners Irish Cider, this BBQ ribs recipe brings orchard vibes straight to your grill. Pork ribs are slow-cooked over gentle heat, kissed with cider spritzes and basted in a sticky apple and honey glaze made from Magners Irish Cider. Paired with a refreshing apple slaw, this one's a crowd-pleaser – ideal for relaxed weekends, garden gatherings or that first cook of autumn.

Prep

Rub the pork lightly with mustard or oil, if using, then coat evenly with BBQ rub on both sides. Let it sit until the rub looks slightly wet and absorbed.

Stabilise your barbecue at 140°C (275°F) with indirect heat and add wood chunks to the coals for smoke. Wait until the smoke runs clean before placing the ribs on.

Combine all the sauce ingredients (except the cayenne) in a saucepan. Simmer over a medium-low heat until reduced by half. Add the cayenne to taste and transfer to a Kilner jar and store until needed.

Combine all the slaw vegetables and fruits in a bowl. In a separate bowl, stir together the mayo, brown sugar and lemon juice. Pour over the slaw and toss until evenly coated. Chill until ready to serve.

Grill

Place the ribs bone-side down on the barbecue. Spritz lightly with Magners Irish Cider every 30 minutes. After 1 hour, brush both sides of the ribs generously with the BBQ sauce. Wrap tightly in parchment paper or foil and return to the barbecue, bone-side down. Cook for another hour until the internal temperature reaches 92°C (198°F) or the ribs probe tender. Remove and leave to rest, wrapped, for 20 minutes.

Serve

Unwrap and slice the pork. Plate half-racks or individual ribs alongside a generous scoop of apple slaw. Offer extra cider glaze on the side for drizzling.

→ **Add Heat:** Stir a spoonful of chipotle paste or smoked paprika into the BBQ sauce for a fiery version.

→ **Crunch Factor:** Add crushed pecans or toasted seeds to the slaw just before serving.

→ **Make Ahead:** The sauce can be prepped days in advance and stored in the fridge.

→ **Pulled Pork Variant:** Use the same rub and sauce with pork shoulder for a pulled-pork twist.

SEAFOOD SEAFOOD SEAFOOD *Seafood*

SOY-GLAZED SCALLOPS with GINGER & SPRING ONION
Sweet heat in the shell

Prep Time: 15 minutes
Cook Time: 4-6 minutes

SERVES 4–6 AS A STARTER (20 scallops)

- 20 fresh scallops in their shells
- Spray vegetable oil

FOR THE SAUCE
- 3 tbsp green spring onions, finely chopped
- 1 tbsp thick soy sauce
- 1 tsp finely chopped fresh green ginger
- 1 tsp finely chopped lemongrass (white part only)
- 1 tbsp lime juice
- 1 small green chilli, deseeded and finely chopped
- ½ tbsp water

Delicate, buttery scallops meet punchy aromatics in this quick-fire barbecue showstopper. Steamed in their own shells over the grill, these scallops are bathed in a bold mix of soy, lime, ginger and lemongrass for a beautifully balanced bite. They're fast, elegant and make a perfect starter or a luxe sharing plate when you want to impress with minimal fuss.

Prep
Carefully open each shell and check the scallops are clean and free from grit. Lift each scallop out, give the inside of the shell a quick spray of oil, and return the scallop to its base. Refrigerate until ready to cook.

In a small bowl, combine the chopped spring onions, soy sauce, ginger, lemongrass, lime juice, chilli and water. Stir well.

Spoon a small amount of the sauce over each scallop in its shell – just enough to coat.

Grill
Place the scallops, still in their shells, directly onto a medium-hot barbecue grill (180–230°C/350–450°F). Work in batches if needed. Cook for 2–3 minutes, then either gently flip the scallop within the shell or rotate the shell slightly to cook evenly.

Spoon a little extra sauce over each scallop near the end of cooking. Remove once the scallops are just opaque and cooked through.

Serve
Serve immediately with lime wedges and a cold beer or crisp white wine.

Cooking without the shell:

Prep
In a small bowl, combine the spring onions, soy sauce, ginger, lemongrass, lime juice, chilli and water. Stir well and set aside.

Heat a cast-iron skillet, griddle plate or soapstone over a medium-high heat. Lightly oil the surface to prevent sticking.

Grill
Toss the scallops with a tablespoon of oil and place them onto the hot surface. Sear for 1½–2 minutes per side until they develop a golden crust and are just opaque in the centre. Avoid overcrowding – cook in batches if needed.

In the final 30 seconds of cooking, spoon or brush the sauce over the scallops, allowing it to sizzle and slightly reduce. Flip them once more to coat evenly.

Serve
Transfer to a serving plate and drizzle any leftover sauce from the pan over the top. Garnish with extra chopped spring onion or coriander, if desired.

→ **Make It A Platter:** Serve scallops on a bed of grilled greens like bok choy or Chinese broccoli for a full barbecue plate.

→ **Add Crunch:** Garnish with crispy shallots or toasted sesame seeds for texture and extra flavour.

→ **Spice Variations:** Swap green chilli for red for more heat, or use a dash of sesame oil in the sauce for a richer profile.

→ **Serve With:** Steamed rice or grilled skewered prawns to build a full barbecue spread.

CAJUN-STYLE FISH with SEARED PINEAPPLE SALSA

Sweet heat on the grill

Prep Time: 15 minutes
Cook Time: 10–12 minutes

SERVES 4

4 boneless fish fillets (such as cod, haddock or sea bass)

Neutral oil, for greasing the skillet

FOR THE CAJUN RUB

1 tbsp paprika

1 tbsp light brown sugar

1 tsp garlic powder

1 tsp sea salt

½ tsp dried thyme

½ tsp dried oregano

½ tsp celery salt

½ tsp onion powder

½ tsp mustard powder

FOR THE SEARED PINEAPPLE SALSA

1 ripe pineapple, peeled and cut into thick rings

1 tbsp rapeseed oil

½ small red onion, finely diced

Juice of 3 limes

2 tbsp finely chopped fresh coriander

½ tsp sea salt

¼ tsp ground cumin

½ red jalapeño, finely diced

This dish brings big Southern flavour to the fire. Fillets are rubbed with a smoky Cajun spice blend, seared in a cast-iron skillet until blackened and crisp at the edges, then paired with a zesty, tropical pineapple salsa that balances sweet, sour and heat. It's bold, bright and made to be eaten outdoors, fresh off the barbecue.

Prep

In a small bowl, combine all the rub ingredients. Mix well. Pat the fish fillets dry and generously coat on both sides with the Cajun mix.

Set your barbecue for direct medium heat (180–230°C/350–450°F). Place a cast-iron pan or skillet on the grill to preheat.

Grill

Lightly oil the skillet. Once hot, sear the fillets for 3–4 minutes per side, or until the outside forms a dark, slightly blackened crust. The internal temperature should reach 60°C (140°F) and the fish should flake easily.

Lightly brush the pineapple slices with rapeseed oil and grill them over direct heat until charred and caramelised – about 2–3 minutes per side. Remove from the grill, let cool slightly, then dice.

In a bowl, combine the diced pineapple, red onion, lime juice, chopped coriander, salt, cumin and red jalapeño. Mix gently and set aside.

Serve

Plate the Cajun fish with a generous spoonful of the seared pineapple salsa over the top or on the side. Serve alongside Southern-style BBQ potatoes for the full experience.

→ **Change the Protein:** This rub and salsa combo also works brilliantly with chicken thighs or shrimp.

→ **Fruit Swap:** Try grilling mango or peaches in place of pineapple for a seasonal twist.

→ **Make It A Taco:** Flake the Cajun fish and serve in warm tortillas with the pineapple salsa and a dollop of soured cream.

→ **Cool It Down:** Add diced avocado or cucumber to the salsa to mellow the heat and add creaminess.

→ **Campfire Hack:** Cook the fish and salsa in foil packets over hot coals if you're off-grid or skipping the skillet.

BBQ SHRIMP with MANGO LIME VINAIGRETTE

Zingy, zesty, fire-kissed

 Prep Time: 15 minutes, plus 30-60 minutes marinating

 Cook Time: 5 minutes

 Equipment: Metal or bamboo skewers (bamboo soaked for 30 minutes)

SERVES 4

- 4 tbsp rapeseed oil
- 1 tsp sea salt
- 1 tsp garlic granules
- ½ tsp freshly ground black pepper
- ½ tsp cayenne pepper
- 900g (2lb) large raw prawns, peeled and deveined

FOR THE MANGO LIME VINAIGRETTE

- ½ ripe mango, peeled, stoned and roughly chopped
- 4 tbsp rapeseed oil
- Handful of fresh coriander, leaves and stems
- 1 spring onion, white part only
- 1 tbsp fresh lime juice
- 1 tbsp rice vinegar
- 1cm (½in) piece of fresh ginger, peeled and chopped
- ½ tsp sea salt
- ¼ tsp freshly ground black pepper

This recipe brings a blast of tropical sunshine to the grill. Juicy prawns are marinated in a bold mix of garlic, cayenne and sea salt before hitting the fire for a smoky char. But the real magic? A vibrant mango and lime vinaigrette that's part salsa, part dressing – bursting with ginger, coriander and zingy citrus. It's light, fresh and made to impress on a warm evening with a cold drink in hand.

Prep

In a large bowl, prepare the marinade. Mix the oil, salt, garlic granules, pepper and cayenne. Add the prawns, toss to coat thoroughly, then cover and marinate in the fridge for 30–60 minutes.

While the prawns marinate, combine all the vinaigrette ingredients in a blender or food processor. Blitz until smooth – about 1 minute. Taste and adjust the seasoning if needed.

Set aside.

Thread the marinated prawns onto skewers. Discard any excess marinade.

Set your barbecue for direct high heat (230–290°C/450–550°F).

Grill

Grill the prawns over the flames with the lid closed, around 2 minutes per side or until just pink, lightly charred and cooked through.

Serve

Plate the prawns straight off the grill and drizzle with plenty of the mango lime vinaigrette. Serve with extra vinaigrette on the side for dipping or spooning over salad, rice or grilled veg.

→ **Turn It into Tacos:** Serve the grilled prawns in warm tortillas with shredded cabbage and a drizzle of the vinaigrette for next-level barbecue tacos.

→ **Add Some Heat:** Blend a small red chilli into the vinaigrette for a spicy version.

→ **No BBQ? No Problem:** These prawns cook just as well under a hot grill or in a grill pan.

→ **Bulk It Up:** Add grilled pineapple chunks or avocado wedges to your serving platter to stretch this into a full meal.

→ **Make It A Platter:** Serve with coconut rice, charred lime wedges and a crisp cucumber salad for a well-rounded summer feast.

SURF & TURF FEAST – RIBEYE, PRAWNS & MUSSELS ON THE GRILL

A BBQ crowd-pleaser that brings land and sea together in perfect harmony

 Prep Time: 30 minutes

 Cook Time: 20–25 minutes

 Equipment: Metal or bamboo skewers (bamboo soaked for 30 minutes)

SERVES 4 AS A HEARTY MAIN OR 6 AS A SHARED FEAST

FOR THE SURF

- 12–16 large raw prawns, peeled, heads and shells removed, deveined
- 1kg (2¼lb) fresh mussels, cleaned and debearded
- 1 shallot, finely chopped
- 2 garlic cloves, finely chopped
- 1 celery stick, finely chopped
- 1 tbsp olive oil
- 300ml (10fl oz) dry cider or white wine
- Bouquet garni (thyme, bay leaves, parsley tied together or loose)
- 200ml (7fl oz) double cream
- Garlic bread wedges, toasted on the grill, to serve

FOR THE TURF

- 1 large ribeye steak (approx. 350–400g/12–14oz)
- Steak seasoning of choice (such as SPG – salt, pepper, garlic)

FOR THE CHILLI-LIME BUTTER

- 150g (5oz) butter, room temperature
- 1 jalapeño, finely chopped
- 1 tbsp chipotle chilli flakes or seasoning
- Zest and juice of 1 lime

This Surf and Turf spread stars a juicy ribeye steak grilled to medium perfection, spicy prawn skewers basted in chilli-lime butter and a pot of cider-steamed mussels finished with cream and herbs. Serve it all with toasted garlic bread for the ultimate sharing platter straight off the grill.

Prep

Start with the chilli-lime butter. In a bowl, combine the butter with the chopped jalapeño, chipotle seasoning, lime zest and juice. Blitz it together with a stick blender or mix by hand until smooth. Set aside.

Thread the cleaned prawns onto skewers. Rinse the mussels under cold water, scrubbing the shells and removing any beards. Discard any mussels that are cracked or stay open when tapped.

Season your ribeye generously with SPG or your chosen rub.

Grill

Grill the steak over direct heat (230–290°C/450–550°F) on the barbecue until it hits an internal temperature of 54°C (129°F) for medium (adjust for your preference – rare would be 45°C (113°F) and well done 65°C (145°F)). Rest for 5–10 minutes before slicing.

Grill the prawn skewers directly over high heat for 2–3 minutes per side or until pink and cooked through. Baste generously with the chilli-lime butter throughout the cook.

In a heavy pan on the barbecue, heat a little oil and soften the shallot, garlic and celery for a few minutes. Add the cleaned mussels, pour in the cider or wine and drop in the bouquet garni. Cover with a lid or foil and steam for 5–6 minutes, or until all the mussel shells have opened. Discard any that remain closed. Stir in the cream and cook for another minute.

While everything finishes cooking, grill slices or wedges of garlic bread over the barbecue until golden and crisp.

Serve

Plate up the sliced ribeye steak, grilled prawn skewers and a generous bowl of creamy mussels. Serve with plenty of warm garlic bread to mop up those buttery, herby juices.

→ **Swap the Prawns:** Use scallops or langoustines for a fancier take, or squid for a seaside Mediterranean vibe.
→ **Make It Smoky:** Add a small wood chunk or a handful of wood chips to your coals for a light smoke that enhances both steak and shellfish.
→ **Extra Heat:** Add a spoonful of harissa or hot sauce to the butter if you like it spicy.
→ **Campfire Version:** Wrap the mussels in foil packets with the veg, herbs, cider and cream. Seal and cook over hot embers for about 10 minutes.
→ **Surf & Turf Burger:** Slice the steak and prawns and serve inside a toasted brioche bun with garlic mayo and a dollop of chilli butter.

BBQ LOBSTER TAILS *with* TROPICAL SALSA
A taste of coastal indulgence

Prep Time: 20 minutes

Cook Time: 10–12 minutes

SERVES 4 AS A MAIN OR 6 AS A SHARED STARTER

4 lobster tails
90g (3oz) unsalted butter, softened
2 tsp freshly crushed garlic
1 tsp lemon pepper seasoning
2 tbsp finely chopped fresh coriander
Oil, for greasing
1 lime, cut into wedges
Sweet chilli sauce, for brushing

FOR THE TROPICAL SALSA

1 large ripe avocado, diced
2 small cucumbers, peeled and diced
1 mango, peeled, stoned and diced
Juice of 1 lemon
2 tbsp finely chopped red onion
60ml (2½fl oz) sweet chilli sauce

This dish is all about surf, smoke and sunshine. BBQ lobster tails are a luxurious yet surprisingly simple way to impress, especially when paired with a refreshing tropical salsa that bursts with creamy avocado, juicy mango and a sweet chilli kick. Fresh lime and herby garlic butter bring the whole dish together with bold, zesty flavour. It's a coastal feast, straight from the grill.

Prep

In a mixing bowl, gently combine the diced avocado, cucumber and mango. Drizzle over the lemon juice to prevent browning, then stir in the red onion and sweet chilli sauce. Cover and refrigerate until ready to serve.

Using kitchen scissors, carefully cut along the top of the lobster tails to expose the flesh within. This will create a small void for us to add the butter.

In a small bowl, mix the softened butter with the garlic, lemon pepper and chopped coriander until fully combined. Coat the exposed lobster meat with the garlic butter using a spoon or brush.

Set your barbecue up for direct heat cooking over high heat (230–290°C/450–550°F). Oil the grill grates well to prevent sticking.

Grill

Place the lobster tails cut-side down on the grill and sear for 2–3 minutes. Flip them to shell-side down and continue grilling for 5–8 minutes, until the shells are bright red and the meat is opaque and firm but not dry. Brush the lobster meat with more garlic butter halfway through, then again just before removing from the grill.

While the lobsters are cooking, place the lime wedges on the grill, cut-side down. Grill until lightly charred, then brush with a little sweet chilli sauce for added flair.

Serve

Transfer the cooked lobster tails to a platter and top each with a final dollop of garlic butter. Garnish with the grilled lime wedges and serve with generous spoonfuls of the tropical salsa.

→ **Make It A Feast:** Serve with grilled corn on the cob brushed with lime butter or a bowl of coconut rice to stretch the meal.

→ **Spicy Upgrade:** Add finely chopped red chilli to the garlic butter for a fiery twist, or stir a spoonful of sriracha into the salsa.

→ **Fresh Herb Swap:** Use flat-leaf parsley or Thai basil for a different aromatic angle.

→ **Smoked Flavour Boost:** Toss a few wood chips onto the coals before grilling for smoky flavour.

CALIFORNIA-INSPIRED FISH TACOS with AVOCADO CREMA

Cali sunshine wrapped in a warm tortilla

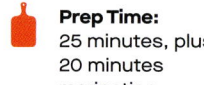

Prep Time: 25 minutes, plus 20 minutes marinating

Cook Time: 10 minutes

SERVES 4–6

| 1 tsp chilli powder |
| 1 tbsp olive oil |
| Zest and juice of 3 limes |
| 450g (1lb) snapper or cod fillets |
| 1 ripe avocado, peeled and stoned |
| 240g (8½oz) Mexican crema or crème fraîche |
| Small bunch of fresh coriander, roughly chopped |
| 12 jalapeños |
| 8–12 corn or flour tortillas |
| Sea salt and freshly ground black pepper |

TO SERVE

| Lime wedges |
| Pickled red onions |
| Fresh coriander leaves |
| Crumbled feta |
| Hot sauces |

Our visit to California – especially the food truck scene – left a serious mark on my taco game. Tacos there aren't just a snack, they're a culture. I remember standing in line at a truck, the smell of grilled fish and lime wafting through the air, and a table full of bright pickled veg, blistered chillies and creamy sauces ready for the taking.

This fish taco recipe captures that spirit – charred white fish, fresh lime, creamy avocado-laced crema and grilled tortillas served DIY-style. There's something about flaking perfectly grilled fish into a warm taco that makes everything feel right. Set it up like they do – big bowls of toppings, cold beers on ice – and let everyone build their own. Perfect for barbecue nights or laidback weekends that feel like a California sunset.

Prep
In a small bowl, whisk together the chilli powder, oil and half the lime zest and juice. Pour over the fish in a shallow dish. Season with salt and pepper, cover, then put in the fridge to marinate for 20 minutes.

In a blender, combine the avocado, crema, remaining lime zest and juice and coriander. Blitz until smooth and silky. Season to taste and chill.

Heat your barbecue to medium-high (180–230°C/350–450°F).

Grill
Grill the jalapeños for about 4 minutes, turning until blistered and charred. Remove and set aside.

Grill the fish fillets for 3–4 minutes per side, depending on thickness, until just cooked and lightly charred. Transfer to a plate and tent with foil.

Quickly warm the tortillas, about 1 minute per side, then wrap in a clean towel to keep warm.

Serve
Flake the fish into large pieces and serve it all family-style: warm tortillas, flaked fish, avocado crema, grilled jalapeños and all the toppings. Let guests build their own tacos.

→ **Baja-Style:** Add a crisp cabbage slaw with lime and cumin for that classic fish taco crunch.
→ **Spicy Crema:** Blend a roasted jalapeño or chipotle in adobo into the crema.
→ **Tropical Twist:** Top with grilled pineapple chunks or mango salsa.
→ **No Grill?** Use a hot cast-iron skillet for both fish and tortillas.

SEAFOOD

GOLD COAST-INSPIRED COCONUT & LIME SHRIMP SKEWERS

Bright, beachy and dangerously snackable

 Prep Time:
15 minutes, plus 30 minutes–2 hours marinating

 Cook Time:
4–6 minutes

 Equipment:
Metal or bamboo skewers (bamboo soaked for 30 minutes)

SERVES 4–6

- 900g (2lb) raw prawns, heads removed and tails on
- 400ml (14fl oz) tin of unsweetened coconut milk
- 1 tbsp yellow curry powder or Thai-style red curry paste
- 1 tbsp ground turmeric
- 1 tbsp minced fresh ginger
- 1 tbsp finely chopped lemongrass
- 1 tsp dried chilli flakes, or finely sliced red chilli
- 3 tbsp fish sauce
- 35g (1½oz) desiccated coconut or coconut flakes
- Fresh lime wedges, for squeezing

This dish takes me back to the sun-soaked sands of the Gold Coast in Australia, where prawns are almost a way of life and cooking over fire is second nature. We found ourselves in a lovely beachside restaurant that was serving grilled skewers of prawns scented with lime, lemongrass and coconut – the aroma alone was unforgettable. These grilled prawn skewers bring that Queensland spirit straight to the barbecue. Marinated in coconut milk, lemongrass and chilli, then grilled to perfection on a barbecue plancha, soapstone or skillet, they're vibrant, bold and unmistakably coastal. Finished with a small pinch of flaky sea salt, they are perfect with a chilled Sauvignon Blanc, and even better with the sound of ocean waves crashing nearby.

Prep

Rinse the prawns under cold running water and pat dry with kitchen paper.

In a bowl, whisk together the coconut milk, curry powder or paste, turmeric, ginger, lemongrass, chilli and fish sauce. Stir in the coconut. Add the prawns to the marinade and toss to coat. Cover and refrigerate for at least 30 minutes, or up to 2 hours.

Thread the prawns onto the soaked skewers and brush lightly with the reserved marinade.

Grill

Place the skewers directly on the grill on a high heat (230–290°C/450–550°F) and cook for about 2 minutes per side, until the prawns are pink, firm and opaque.

Serve

Serve on a bed of grilled pineapple and rice, with lime wedges on the side.

→ **Street Food-Style:** Serve with a spicy sweet chilli dipping sauce or a fresh mango salsa.
→ **Tropical Aussie Vibes:** Add chunks of grilled pineapple or green mango to the skewers.
→ **Surf Club Twist:** Serve over avocado-lime slaw or wrap in a warm flatbread with a slather of coconut yoghurt.

CEDAR-PLANKED TERIYAKI SALMON

Marinated, smoked and fire-kissed

Prep Time: 15 minutes, plus 1 hour marinating

Cook Time: 15–20 minutes

Equipment: 1 untreated cedar plank

SERVES 4–6

- 1 side of salmon (approx. 1–1.2kg/2¼–2¾lb), skin on and pin bones removed
- Olive oil or rapeseed oil, for brushing
- Sea salt and freshly ground black pepper
- Fresh herbs, sesame seeds and lemon or lime wedges, to serve

FOR THE TERIYAKI MARINADE

- 6 tbsp soy sauce
- 4 tbsp maple syrup
- 2 tbsp mirin (rice wine)
- 4 garlic cloves, finely sliced
- 4cm (1½in) piece of fresh ginger, finely sliced

This one's a crowd favourite from my BBQ classes. Cedar-planked salmon is all about layering flavour. Instead of brushing on a glaze during the cook, the salmon is marinated in a homemade teriyaki mix featuring soy sauce, maple syrup, mirin, ginger and garlic. As it cooks gently on a smouldering cedar plank, the fish soaks in sweet, savoury and smoky notes – perfect for a showstopping barbecue main with very little fuss and served directly on the smouldering plank!

Prep

In a bowl or sealable bag, mix together the soy sauce, maple syrup, mirin, sliced garlic and ginger. No need to cook it – this version is raw and ready to marinate.

Place the salmon in a shallow dish or bag, flesh-side down in the marinade. Cover and refrigerate for 30 minutes to 1 hour, turning once, if needed, to coat evenly. Avoid marinating for longer than 2 hours, to prevent the fish becoming too soft from the acidity.

While the salmon marinates, soak the cedar plank in cold water for at least 1 hour. This keeps it from burning and allows it to smoulder gently on the grill.

Set your barbecue for indirect cooking at 180–200°C (350–400°F). Place the cedar plank over direct heat for 2–3 minutes until it starts to smoke, then move it to the cooler side of the grill.

Remove the salmon from the marinade and let any excess drip off. Place skin-side down on the plank. Discard the used marinade. Lightly brush the salmon with oil and season with a touch of salt and pepper.

Grill

Close the lid and cook the salmon for 15–20 minutes, until it flakes easily with a fork and reaches an internal temperature of 50–52°C (122–125°F) for medium. The cedar plank will release aromatic smoke as it gently cooks the fish.

Serve

Carefully remove the cedar plank from the grill and serve the salmon directly from it. Garnish with fresh herbs or a few sesame seeds, and lemon or lime wedges on the side.

→ **Extra Glaze:** If you want a sticky finish, simmer a second batch of the marinade (or reserved portion) until thickened, then brush it on during the last 5 minutes.

→ **Add A Kick:** Stir in a teaspoon of sriracha or finely chopped red chilli to the marinade.

LAMB
AMB
LAMB
LAM
Lamb

Lamb

LAMB

LAMB

LAMB

LAMB

STICKY APRICOT & MUSTARD-GLAZED LAMB CHOPS

A magical blend of earthy spices, sweet fruits and charred lamb

Prep Time: 15 minutes, plus 30 minutes marinating

 Cook Time: 20 minutes

SERVES 4

| 2 racks of lamb (approx. 1kg/2¼lb each), French trimmed (ask your butcher to do this) |
| 2 tsp flaky sea salt |
| 1½ tsp freshly ground black pepper |

FOR THE GLAZE

| 200g (7oz) apricot jam |
| 3 tbsp wholegrain mustard |
| 4 tbsp extra virgin olive oil |
| 1 tbsp fresh lemon juice, cider vinegar or white wine vinegar (optional for balance) |
| 3 tbsp fresh thyme leaves, finely chopped |
| 6 garlic cloves, minced |
| Zest of 1 lemon |
| ½ tsp ground cinnamon |
| ¼ tsp smoked paprika |

Inspired by the lamb we tasted in a Moroccan restaurant, this dish completely flipped the switch on how I think about pairing fruit with red meat. This barbecue version brings that inspiration home – racks of lamb glazed in sticky apricot jam, mustard, garlic and thyme, with a touch of warming spices to round it out. It's simple but sings with flavour, and it's perfect for when you want to show off a bit at the grill.

Prep

In a bowl, stir together the apricot jam, mustard, olive oil, lemon juice or vinegar, thyme, garlic, lemon zest, cinnamon and smoked paprika. You're looking for a thick, punchy glaze with a sweet-savoury edge. Spoon a few tablespoons into a small bowl and keep that for later – it's your finishing touch.

Take your lamb racks and slather them all over with the glaze – go heavier on the meaty side. Let them sit out at room temperature for 20–30 minutes so the flavours can really settle in. Just before they hit the grill, season generously with sea salt and freshly ground black pepper.

Fire up your barbecue for a medium-heat cook (about 200°C/400°F). You want a nice even heat – not raging flames – so if you're using charcoal, go for a steady base of heat rather than a firestorm.

Grill

Lay the lamb racks bone-side down on the grill. Keep the lid closed as much as possible to trap the heat, and turn them every so often for even cooking and colour. Keep an eye out – with the sugars in the glaze, things can caramelise fast.

Cook for around 20 minutes, or until the internal temperature hits about 52–54°C (125–130°F) for medium rare, then lift them off and brush them with that reserved glaze. Let them rest under foil for 5–10 minutes – this step makes all the difference to juicy chops.

Serve

Slice the racks into single chops and pile them up on a board. Finish with a scattering of herbs or serve with your favourite sides – grilled veg, spiced grains or just a cold beer.

→ **Kick of Heat:** Add a spoonful of harissa to the glaze for a kick.
→ **Creamy Contrast:** Serve alongside a cucumber-yoghurt dip or whipped feta for contrast.
→ **Twist It Up:** Swap apricot jam for peach or fig preserves for a seasonal twist.

SUNDAY ROAST BBQ LAMB *with* ROAST VEG & YORKSHIRE PUDS

A smoky spin on the classic

 Prep Time: 30 minutes, plus 2 hours or overnight resting and marinating (optional)

 Cook Time: 2–2½ hours

SERVES 6–8

- 5–6 sprigs of fresh rosemary
- 5–6 sprigs of fresh mint
- 4 garlic cloves
- Zest and juice of 1 lemon
- 60ml (2½fl oz) olive oil
- 1 tbsp sea salt (or swap for 2–3 anchovies for umami)
- ½ tbsp freshly ground black pepper
- 1 tsp red wine vinegar or a pinch of smoked paprika (optional)
- 1 whole leg of lamb (approx. 2.2kg/5lb), bone in

FOR THE ROAST VEG

- 4 carrots, peeled and halved lengthways
- 3 parsnips, peeled and halved lengthways
- 2 red onions, cut into quarters
- Beef dripping or neutral oil
- 4 large potatoes, peeled and halved

FOR THE YORKSHIRE PUDDINGS

- 4 eggs
- 200ml (7fl oz) whole milk
- 200g (7oz) plain flour
- Pinch of salt
- Beef dripping, tallow or oil for muffin tin

This one's straight from the heart and the barbecue. A golden, herb-crusted leg of lamb slow-roasted over coals, soaking the tray of root veg below in its glorious drippings, all rounded off with puffed-up Yorkshire puddings that rise to the occasion every time.

Prep

Blitz the rosemary, mint, garlic, lemon zest and juice, olive oil, salt (or anchovies), pepper and your optional extra into a thick paste. Spoon off a couple of tablespoons to use on the veg later.

Score the skin of the lamb in a crisscross pattern to help the rub sink in. Slather the lamb all over with the herb mix, getting right into the cuts. Let it sit for at least 30 minutes at room temperature – or stash it in the fridge for a few hours to deepen the flavour.

To make the Yorkshire pudding batter, whisk together the eggs and milk, then sift in the flour and salt. Mix to a smooth batter, then rest in the fridge for an hour or overnight.

Fire up the barbecue for indirect cooking at around 200°C (400°F).

Grill

Pop all the veg, except the potatoes, into a tray, toss with the reserved herb rub and a good glug of dripping or oil, then position the lamb directly above them on the grill grates. As the lamb roasts, it'll baste the veg with its juices.

Cook until the lamb hits 60°C (140°F) internal temperature for medium (about 1½–2 hours). Once done, take it off the grill and tent it loosely with foil for at least 20 minutes, to rest and reabsorb its juices.

While the lamb is resting, crank your barbecue or oven to 250°C (475°F).

Preheat a muffin tin with fat until smoking hot, then carefully pour in the batter. Bake for 25–30 minutes until golden and puffed – no peeking!

Boil the potatoes for 6 minutes, then drain and let them steam-dry. Toss into hot oil or dripping and roast alongside the lamb or separately until crisp and golden brown.

Serve

Carve thick slices of lamb, stack with golden roasties and caramelised veg, then top with a giant Yorkshire. Drizzle over a proper gravy or go fancy with a minty jus.

→ **Cheesy Twist:** Add grated Cheddar or a spoonful of English mustard to the Yorkshire batter for extra flavour.

LAMB

CURRY YOGHURT LAMB CUTLETS

A backyard take on big festival energy

 Prep Time:
20 minutes, plus 1 hour or overnight marinating

 Cook Time:
6–8 minutes

SERVES 4

- 12 lean lamb cutlets
- Olive oil, for brushing

FOR THE MARINADE

- 110ml (4fl oz) natural yoghurt, plus extra to serve
- 1 tbsp lemon juice
- 2 garlic cloves, crushed
- 1cm (½in) piece of fresh ginger, grated
- 2 tsp curry powder
- ½ tsp ground cumin (optional, for added depth)
- Sea salt and freshly ground black pepper

TO SERVE

- Fresh mint, chopped
- Mango chutney or pomegranate seeds (optional)

This one's straight from the memory bank – Pub in the Park, summer sun and a lamb dish by chef Atul Kochhar that stopped me in my tracks. It was bold, tender and packed with layers of spice mellowed out by creamy yoghurt. Back home, I was inspired to try and recreate it. I gave it the barbecue treatment and it's been a go-to ever since. These lamb cutlets are marinated in a fragrant yoghurt blend, grilled hot and fast, and finished with a dollop of cool yoghurt or chutney. They're fuss-free, full of flavour and always get people asking for the recipe. These cutlets are brilliant on flatbreads or as part of a larger barbecue feast board. Festival vibes, without the overpriced pint.

Prep

In a bowl, stir together the yoghurt, lemon juice, garlic, ginger, curry powder, cumin and a good pinch of salt and pepper. Coat the lamb cutlets generously in the marinade and leave to rest in the fridge for at least an hour. Longer is better – overnight is ideal if you have the time.

Remove the cutlets from the marinade, letting any excess drip off.

Preheat your barbecue to high heat (230–290°C/450–550°F). These cutlets want a quick, direct blast of heat for a charred crust and juicy centre.

Grill

Brush the grill grates with oil, then lay the cutlets down over the flames. Grill for about 3–4 minutes on each side, depending on thickness, until the outside is caramelised and the inside is blushing pink.

Serve

Serve hot off the grill with a generous spoon of natural yoghurt and a sprinkle of fresh mint. A spoonful of mango chutney or a few pomegranate seeds work brilliantly for contrast.

→ **Switch It Up:** Swap lamb for chicken thighs or tenderloins. For a dipping sauce, stir chopped mint and mango chutney into natural yoghurt.

CHILLI LAMB SKEWERS *with* GINGER & SOY SLAW

Light, fiery and full of flavour

 Prep Time: 20 minutes

 Cook Time: 6–8 minutes

 Equipment: 4 metal (lightly oiled) or bamboo skewers (bamboo soaked for 30 minutes)

SERVES 4

500g (17oz) lean lamb strips
½ tsp chilli powder
Spray oil
2 limes, cut in half

FOR THE SLAW

400g (14oz) shredded Chinese cabbage
50g (2oz) finely sliced spring onions
85g (3oz) diced red pepper
60g (2½oz) sugar snap peas
60ml (2½fl oz) low-sodium soy sauce
1 tbsp green ginger, minced
1 small red chilli, seeds in and minced
1 tsp sesame oil
1 tsp palm sugar
2 tbsp lime juice

When you're craving something with a little kick and a lot of crunch, this dish brings it all. Tender lamb skewers spiced with just the right amount of heat meet a crisp, colourful slaw that's bursting with zingy lime, fresh chilli and ginger. It's quick to cook, fun to eat and perfect for everything from weeknight dinners to weekend barbecues. Stack it up, squeeze that lime and get ready for a flavour party on your plate!

Prep
Thread equal amounts of the lamb onto the skewers in an 'S' shape. Sprinkle evenly with the chilli powder and let the meat sit for 5 minutes.

Make the slaw by combining the cabbage, spring onions, pepper and sugar snaps. In a separate container, mix the soy sauce, ginger, chilli, sesame oil, sugar and lime juice. Stir well, then pour over the cabbage mix and toss well.

Grill
Cook the oil-sprayed lamb on a medium-hot (180–230°C/350–450°F) barbecue plate for 5 minutes or leave longer for well done.

Serve
Serve each skewer of lamb on top of equal amounts of slaw and place a lime half on each plate.

HERBY LEMON LAMB KEBABS with WARM FLATBREADS & FIERY GARLIC SAUCE

Simple, smoky and sensational

Prep Time: 20 minutes, plus at least 2 hours marinating

Cook Time: 10–12 minutes

Equipment: 8 metal or bamboo skewers (bamboo soaked for 30 minutes)

SERVES 4

- 750g (1lb 11oz) boneless lamb, cut into roughly 2cm (¾in) cubes
- 120ml (4fl oz) fresh lemon juice
- 2 tsp finely chopped fresh oregano
- 1 tbsp finely chopped fresh parsley
- 2 garlic cloves, finely minced
- 1 small onion, finely chopped
- 2 fresh bay leaves, torn into pieces
- 60ml (2½fl oz) extra virgin olive oil
- Sea salt and freshly ground black pepper

TO SERVE

- Warm flatbreads (see page 157)
- Tabbouleh (see page 59)
- Your favourite chilli garlic sauce
- Extra lemon wedges, to squeeze

Nothing quite captures the laidback joy of grilling like these juicy, herby lamb kebabs. Inspired by my travels around sun-soaked Mediterranean towns, these skewers are vibrant with fresh oregano, zesty lemon and just enough garlic to keep things interesting. Grill them up tender and lightly charred, then pile them generously into soft, warm flatbreads loaded with crunchy tabbouleh salad and a kick of chilli garlic sauce. It's interactive eating at its finest, ideal for sunny weekend gatherings or a flavourful midweek feast. Gather some friends, pass around the flatbreads, and let everyone dive into their own tasty creations.

Prep

Toss the lamb cubes in a mixing bowl with the lemon juice, oregano, parsley, garlic, onion, bay leaves and olive oil. Season generously with sea salt and black pepper. Mix thoroughly, ensuring each lamb cube is coated. Cover and marinate in the fridge for at least 2 hours, or longer if possible, to deepen the flavours.

Once marinated, thread about 5–6 pieces of lamb onto each skewer, spacing evenly to ensure even grilling. Save any leftover marinade for basting – it'll give the lamb extra flavour and a beautiful caramelised crust.

Preheat your barbecue grill or hotplate to a high heat (230–290°C/450–550°F) and brush the grill lightly with oil.

Grill

Place the kebabs directly onto the hot grill, turning every few minutes and brushing frequently with the reserved marinade. Grill for approximately 4–6 minutes per side until golden brown with delicious charred edges – cooked but still tender to the touch. As the kebabs finish up, gently warm your flatbreads on the edge of the grill.

Serve

To serve, grab a warm flatbread and load it generously with tabbouleh salad. Add a kebab skewer's worth of juicy lamb, then finish it off with a generous splash of fiery chilli garlic sauce and an extra squeeze of lemon. Eat immediately with good company, good conversation and something chilled to wash it down.

CHIC
CKEN
Chicken
CHICK

BBQ CHICKEN SHAWARMA

Spit-roasted, spiced and flatbread-ready

 Prep Time: 15 minutes, plus 2–24 hours marinating

 Cook Time: 1–1½ hours (depending on method)

 Feeds a Crowd

SERVES 6–8

- 3 tbsp tomato paste
- 4 garlic cloves, minced
- Zest and juice of 2 lemons
- 2 tsp onion granules
- 2 tsp ground cumin
- 1 tsp ground coriander
- 1 tsp smoked paprika
- ½ tsp ground allspice
- ½ tsp cayenne pepper
- 1 tbsp finely chopped fresh thyme
- 3 tsp sea salt
- 2 tsp freshly ground black pepper
- 8 tbsp olive oil
- 1.8kg (4lb) boneless and skinless chicken thighs

TO SERVE

- Warm flatbreads (see page 157)
- Crisp salad
- Your favourite sauces

Rich with tomato, garlic and warm spices, these marinated chicken thighs are cooked slowly over fire until tender and caramelised on the outside. Whether you're using a rotisserie or stacking them up over indirect heat, this is a shawarma-style barbecue dish that delivers every time – best served straight into homemade flatbreads with your favourite sauces and crisp salad, and perfect for feeding a crowd.

Prep

In a large bowl, whisk together the tomato paste, garlic, lemon zest and juice, onion granules, cumin, coriander, paprika, allspice, cayenne pepper, thyme, salt, pepper and olive oil. Add the chicken thighs and mix well until every piece is thoroughly coated. Use gloves and get your hands in – this is best done by touch. Cover and refrigerate for at least 2 hours, ideally overnight. The longer it marinates, the deeper the flavour.

Prepare your barbecue for indirect cooking at 180–200°C (350–400°F) or attach your rotisserie kit, if using one.

For rotisserie: attach one fork, then slide the chicken thighs on, stacking tightly. Add the second fork to hold the meat snug. For extra control, insert a few metal skewers horizontally through the stack to stabilise the shape.

Grill

Mount the rotisserie and cook over indirect heat, basting occasionally with any leftover marinade. Cook until an internal temperature of 74°C (165°F) is reached.

For non-rotisserie: stack marinated thighs tightly on a vertical skewer or thread them onto flat skewers and cook over indirect heat, turning occasionally.

Serve

Rest briefly, then slice the chicken thinly straight off the spit. Pile into warm flatbreads with crisp salad and your favourite sauces.

➔ **Flavour Boost:** Add smoked paprika or dried chilli flakes to the marinade for a bolder kick.

➔ **Serve With:** Garlic sauce, tahini yoghurt, pickled chillies, cucumber ribbons or grilled veg.

➔ **No Waste:** Can be used cold in wraps, with rice or chopped into salads the next day.

➔ **Make It A Feast:** Pair with grilled halloumi, spiced rice and charred flatbreads for a full spread.

BUFFALO HOT WINGS

Sharp, buttery heat and fire-kissed crunch

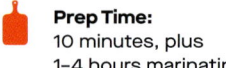
Prep Time:
10 minutes, plus
1–4 hours marinating

Cook Time:
30–40 minutes

SERVES 4

1.25kg (2¾lb) chicken wings

FOR THE DRY RUB

2 tsp celery salt

2 tsp white pepper

1 tsp black pepper

FOR THE BUFFALO SAUCE

1 bottle Frank's RedHot sauce

1 tbsp honey

50g (2oz) unsalted butter

TO SERVE

Ranch dressing or blue cheese dressing

Celery sticks

Crumbled blue cheese (optional)

Sticky, spicy and smoky, these Buffalo hot wings are the real deal. A hit of celery salt in the dry rub brings that traditional Buffalo wing flavour, while cooking over the fire adds depth and char. Tossed in a buttery hot sauce glaze and served with cooling ranch or blue cheese dressing, these are made for tearing into with messy fingers.

Prep
Combine the celery salt with the white and black peppers. Toss the wings in the dry rub until evenly coated. Cover and refrigerate for 1–4 hours to absorb the flavours.

In a saucepan, whisk together the Frank's sauce and honey. Bring to a gentle simmer. Stir in the butter and cook until melted and slightly reduced – about 2 minutes. Set aside, reserving some in a bowl for dipping.

Set your barbecue for direct and indirect zones on a high heat (230–290°C/450–550°F).

Grill
Start the wings over direct heat to get some colour and char, turning occasionally. Move the wings to the indirect zone and cook with the lid closed until the internal temperature hits 75°C (167°F) (but you may wish to push this to 85–90°C/185–194°F to achieve a nice crispy skin). Check the internal temperature using an instant-read thermometer.

Serve
Just before serving, toss the hot wings in the warm Buffalo sauce. Serve immediately with a side of ranch or blue cheese dressing, celery sticks and crumble blue cheese on top, if you like.

→ **Smoked Butter:** Use smoked butter in your sauce for added depth.
→ **Make It Spicier:** Add dried chilli flakes or cayenne to the rub for extra heat.
→ **Sweeten It Up:** Mix in a dash of maple syrup or hot honey for a sweet-spicy twist.
→ **Serve With:** Blue cheese slaw, cornbread or loaded fries.

STICKY PEANUT CHICKEN SKEWERS

BBQ glazed and straight from the grill

 Prep Time: 15 minutes, plus 30 minutes marinating

 Cook Time: 6–8 minutes

 **Equipment:** 12 metal or bamboo skewers (bamboo soaked for 30 minutes)

SERVES 4

- 1 tbsp peanut butter
- 2 tbsp soy sauce
- 2 tbsp lemon juice
- ½ tsp sugar
- 1 garlic clove, crushed
- 1 tbsp sweet chilli sauce
- 500g (17oz) chicken breast or thigh fillets, cut into 2cm (¾in) cubes
- 6 spring onions, white parts cut into 3cm (1¼in) length, green parts reserved and finely sliced
- Jasmine rice, to serve
- Fresh coriander leaves, to garnish

These chicken skewers are a go-to for quick barbecue wins. Tender chunks of chicken are coated in a sweet, nutty marinade with a kick of chilli and citrus, then grilled over flame until sticky and caramelised. Threaded with spring onions for freshness and served over jasmine rice, they're bold, simple and made for sharing.

Prep
In a bowl, mix together the peanut butter, soy sauce, lemon juice, sugar, garlic and sweet chilli sauce until smooth. Add the cubed chicken and mix until coated. Cover and refrigerate for at least 30 minutes.

Thread the chicken pieces onto the skewers, alternating with the white parts of the spring onion.

Grill
Cook the skewers over direct barbecue medium–high heat (180–230°C/350–450°F), turning regularly and brushing with any leftover marinade. Grill for 6–8 minutes or until the chicken is golden, sticky and fully cooked through.

Serve
Plate up over jasmine rice. Garnish with fresh coriander leaves and the finely sliced green ends of the spring onions.

→ **Add Crunch:** Top with crushed peanuts or crispy fried onions before serving.
→ **Switch the Base:** Serve with vermicelli noodles, rice paper wraps or BBQ-grilled flatbreads.
→ **Spice It Up:** Add a teaspoon of sriracha or a splash of hot sauce to the marinade for extra heat.
→ **Make It Veggie:** Swap chicken for tofu or halloumi and adjust cooking times accordingly.
→ **BBQ Tip:** Let the skewers rest for a couple of minutes after cooking to keep the juices locked in.

DYNAMITE POPCORN CHICKEN *with* PICKLED CUCUMBER & FLATBREADS

A dangerous mix of hot and cool

 Prep Time: 20 minutes, plus 1–24 hours marinating

 Cook Time: 15 minutes

Inspired by the fast-paced street food I encountered in the Southern-style chicken joints across the US, but with a Southeast Asian twist. This recipe is a mash-up of flavour and fire. I've slow-brined the chicken in buttermilk and spices to lock in juiciness, then double-coated it and fried it for crunch. The dynamite sauce gives it a spicy slap in the face – in the best way – and the pickled cucumber salad cools it all down again. Wrap it up in flatbreads and you've got a messy, mouthwatering barbecue feast built for sharing.

SERVES 4

500ml (17fl oz) buttermilk
1 tbsp onion powder
1 tbsp garlic powder
1 tbsp sea salt
1 tsp cracked black pepper
450g (1lb) chicken thighs, cut into bite-sized chunks
Oil, for frying

FOR THE DRY COATING

120g (4fl oz) plain flour
120g (4fl oz) cornflour
1 tbsp onion powder
1 tbsp garlic powder
1 tbsp sea salt
1 tsp cracked black pepper

FOR THE SALAD

120ml (4fl oz) rice vinegar
1 tsp sesame oil
1 tsp soy sauce
2 tsp minced garlic
1 tsp sugar
1 cucumber, thinly sliced

FOR THE DYNAMITE SAUCE

240ml (8fl oz) mayonnaise
1 tbsp chilli garlic sauce
2 tsp sriracha
60ml (2½fl oz) sweet chilli sauce

TO SERVE

Flatbreads (see page 157)
Fresh coriander (optional)

Prep

In a large bowl, combine the buttermilk with the onion and garlic powders, salt and pepper. Add the chicken pieces, cover and refrigerate for at least 1 hour, or preferably overnight.

In another bowl, combine the flour, cornflour, onion and garlic powders, salt and pepper.

To make the salad, whisk together the vinegar, sesame oil, soy sauce, garlic and sugar in a bowl. Toss in the cucumber slices, then cover and let them sit in the fridge to pickle until ready to serve the chicken.

Mix together the mayo, chilli garlic sauce, sriracha and sweet chilli sauce in a bowl until smooth.

Heat just enough oil for shallow frying (about 2.5cm/1in) in a carbon-steel skillet or deep fryer to 200°C (400°F). If using a ceramic kamado-style barbecue, set it up with the half-moon pan over direct heat. If you don't have the proper heat-proof equipment or aren't confident doing this on a BBQ, you can easily do this on your hob.

Remove the chicken from the buttermilk, let the excess drip off, and toss in the dry mix until fully coated.

Grill

Fry the chicken in batches for 4–5 minutes or until crispy and golden, and the internal temperature hits at least 75°C (167°F). Drain on a wire rack.

Serve

Toss the hot chicken in the dynamite sauce until fully coated. Serve immediately in flatbreads with the pickled cucumber and a scattering of coriander, if you're feeling fancy.

→ **Korean Vibe:** Swap sriracha for gochujang in the sauce and top with kimchi.

→ **Tex-Mex Flair:** Serve with grilled corn and chipotle mayo on the side.

FLATBREADS

Prep Time:
15 minutes, plus 30 minutes rest

Cook Time:
1–2 minutes until puffed up and charred to desired level

MAKES 4 MEDIUM FLATBREADS

125g (4½oz) self-raising flour, plus extra for dusting

240ml (8fl oz) Greek yoghurt

Pinch of sea salt

Melted butter, for brushing

There's nothing like wrapping saucy, crispy chicken in a warm, fluffy flatbread straight off the grill. These are dead easy – two base ingredients, no proving, no fuss. Perfect for soaking up that dynamite sauce and catching all the drips.

Prep
Combine the flour, Greek yoghurt and salt in a bowl and mix into a soft dough. Cover and let it rest for 10 minutes – just enough time to get the grill or skillet piping hot.

Divide the dough into 4 pieces. Roll out each ball on a floured surface into rough rounds about 5mm (¼in) thick. Cook them in a dry cast-iron skillet, plancha or directly on a hot barbecue surface for 1–2 minutes per side until golden and slightly puffed.

Serve
Brush the hot breads with melted butter right before serving.

SPICED CHICKEN SKEWERS *with* LEMON-MINT YOGHURT

Fragrant flames, chilled sauce and grilled goodness

 Prep Time: 30 minutes, plus 4 hours marinating

 Cook Time: 8–10 minutes

 **Equipment:** Metal or bamboo skewers (bamboo soaked for 30 minutes)

This one takes me back to wandering the maze-like souks of Marrakech, where the scent of spices and fresh herbs seemed to follow you down every alleyway. Inspired by a chicken skewer that stopped us in our tracks, this version brings together a bold North African-style marinade and a cooling lemon-mint yoghurt sauce.

Grilled over open flames, served with charred veg and dunked into creamy yoghurt, it's sunshine cooking with a spicy soul.

SERVES 4

- 4 boneless and skinless chicken breasts (approx. 175g/6oz each), cut into 4cm (1½in) chunks
- 1 green and 1 red pepper, chopped into 4cm (1½in) pieces
- 1 small red onion, cut into wedges and layers separated
- Warm flatbreads and lemon wedges, to serve

FOR THE MARINADE

- 4 tbsp olive oil
- 3 tbsp chopped fresh coriander
- 3 tbsp chopped fresh mint
- Juice of 1 lemon
- 2 tsp honey
- 1 tsp smoked paprika
- 1 tsp ground cumin
- 2 garlic cloves, crushed
- ½ tsp ground coriander
- ½ tsp ground cinnamon
- ¼ tsp cayenne pepper
- 1½ tsp sea salt

FOR THE YOGHURT SAUCE

- 475ml (16fl oz) full-fat Greek yoghurt
- Zest and juice of 1 lemon
- 3 tbsp chopped fresh mint
- 2 garlic cloves, finely minced
- 1 tsp sea salt

Prep

Whisk all the marinade ingredients together in a bowl. Add the chicken and massage to coat all the chunks. Cover and let it rest in the fridge for at least 4 hours.

Stir together all the yoghurt sauce ingredients in a bowl, then cover and refrigerate until ready to serve. The longer it sits, the better it gets.

Thread the chicken, peppers and onion onto your skewers. Don't overcrowd them – leave a little space between each chunk to help them char nicely.

Preheat your barbecue to medium-high heat (180–230°C/ 350–450°F) with 2 zones (direct and indirect).

Grill

Grill the kebabs directly over the heat, lid down, for a few minutes until seared, then move them to indirect heat for another 8–10 minutes, or until the internal temperature probes 75°C (167°F). You're looking for nicely browned edges and cooked-through chicken. Let the skewers rest for a couple of minutes.

Serve

Serve with a generous spoonful of the lemon-mint yoghurt, warm flatbreads and maybe a squeeze of extra lemon.

➔ **Extra Bite:** Add grilled halloumi or courgette chunks to the skewers for more texture.

➔ **Wrap It Up:** Turn this into a wrap night – serve with flatbreads, shredded lettuce and pickled onions.

➔ **No Waste:** Leftover yoghurt sauce is perfect as a dip or sandwich spread.

SRIRACHA & LIME GRILLED CHICKEN WINGS

Spicy, sweet and citrusy

 Prep Time: 20 minutes, plus 4–12 hours marinating

 Cook Time: 20–25 minutes

SERVES 4–6

| 24 chicken wings |
| 60ml (2½fl oz) sriracha |
| 60ml (2½fl oz) chilli garlic sauce |
| 180ml (6fl oz) honey |
| 125ml (4fl oz) toasted sesame oil |
| 2 limes, cut into quarters |
| 6 lime leaves, shredded |
| 1 small onion, roughly chopped |
| Sea salt and freshly ground black pepper |
| 1 tbsp black sesame seeds, to garnish |
| Tangerine wedges, to serve |

There's just something unbeatable about the energy of a summer barbecue when the wings hit the grill – that sizzle, the sticky glaze and the inevitable crowd hovering nearby. The base is all about bold flavours: sriracha and chilli garlic sauce for heat, honey to balance it all out and plenty of lime. What takes this over the top is the final grill – caramelised edges, juicy interior and the tang of fresh tangerine to finish. These wings are pure flavour bombs, perfect to stash in a cooler for the beach grill.

Prep
If desired, split the wings into the drums and flats. Place in a large dish or bowl.

In a blender, combine the sriracha, chilli garlic sauce, honey, sesame oil, lime quarters, shredded lime leaves and onion. Blitz until smooth. Season with salt and pepper to taste.

Pour the marinade over the wings and toss well to coat. Cover and refrigerate for at least 4 hours, or overnight if you can – the flavour payoff is worth the extra time.

Preheat your barbecue or grill to medium-high (180–230°C/350–450°F) with direct and indirect zones.

Grill
Place the wings on the grill and cook for 6–8 minutes, turning occasionally – the objective being to add colour and some char on the wings. Then move the wings to the indirect side or reduce the heat and continue grilling until fully cooked. I tend to find that they are best pushed past the 75°C (167°F) safe eating point and closer to 90°C (194°F) for fall-off-the-bone meat with crispy skin. Turn occasionally, and check they are cooked through with an instant-read thermometer.

Serve
Pile the wings onto a large platter, sprinkle with black sesame seeds, and serve with fresh tangerine wedges for a sweet, citrusy pop.

➜ **Add Extra Heat:** Sprinkle with a pinch of crushed Thai chilli.
➜ **Make It Funky:** Swap chilli garlic sauce for a spoonful of miso paste and extra sriracha for a funkier twist.
➜ **Final Polish:** Finish with a brush of glaze (made from reduced leftover marinade) before serving.

SPATCHCOCK CHICKEN with GARLIC HERB BUTTER

Crispy skin, juicy centre – pure backyard roast vibes

 Prep Time: 20 minutes, plus 1-2 hours marinating (optional)

 Cook Time: 35-45 minutes (depending on size of bird)

SERVES 4

1 whole chicken (1.5–1.8kg/3¼–4lb)

2 tbsp olive oil

1 tsp sea salt

1 tsp freshly ground black pepper

1 tsp smoked paprika

Zest of 1 lemon, plus wedges to serve

Fresh herbs, to garnish

FOR THE GARLIC HERB BUTTER

100g (3½oz) unsalted butter, softened

3 garlic cloves, minced

1 tbsp chopped fresh rosemary

1 tbsp chopped fresh thyme

1 tbsp chopped flat-leaf parsley

1 tsp Dijon mustard

Juice of ½ lemon

Pinch of sea salt and freshly ground black pepper

There's just something primal and satisfying about throwing a whole bird on the barbecue, especially when it's spatchcocked for faster, more even cooking. It feels like a proper feast, but without the faff. This version dials up the flavour with a punchy garlic and herb butter that's worked under the skin and brushed over the flames as it grills. What you get is golden, smoky skin, juicy meat that practically falls apart and a table full of people reaching in for more. It's rustic, bold and perfect for feeding a hungry crowd – no carving skills required.

Prep

Place your chicken breast-side down on a board. Using sharp kitchen shears, cut out the backbone (discard or save it for stock). Flip over the bird and press down firmly with your palm until the breastbone cracks and the bird flattens. Pat it dry all over with kitchen paper.

Drizzle with the olive oil, then season with the salt, pepper, smoked paprika and lemon zest. If you have time, leave it uncovered in the fridge for an hour or two – this helps to dry the skin and produces crispier results.

In a small bowl, mix the softened butter with the garlic, herbs, mustard, lemon juice and seasoning. Lift the skin gently away from the breast and thighs and smear some of the butter underneath. Save the rest for basting.

Set your barbecue for indirect cooking at 180–200°C (350–400°F) with the lid closed, coals banked to one side or burners turned off in the middle.

Grill

Place the chicken skin-side up over the indirect zone. Close the lid and cook for 30–35 minutes.

Flip the bird, skin-side down, over the hot side of the grill for 5–10 minutes to crisp up the skin. Keep a close eye – it should blister and brown, not burn. Baste generously with the remaining herb butter while it cooks.

Serve

Once the internal temperature of the thickest part of the thigh hits 75°C (167°F), take it off the grill and rest for 10 minutes, loosely tented with foil. Carve into halves or quarters and serve with lemon wedges and a fresh herb garnish.

→ **Add A Kick:** Add a teaspoon of dried chilli flakes or harissa to the herb butter.

→ **Smoky Notes:** Toss in a chunk of cherry or apple wood when setting up the barbecue. Chicken is easy to over-smoke, so go sparingly with the added wood – sweet fruit woods work best in my experience.

THE PERFECT SHARING STEAK

BBQ nights, weekend feasts, steak done right

Nothing beats slicing into a massive, flame-kissed steak and sharing it with friends or family. Instead of juggling individual steaks, go big and bold with something like a 1.6kg (3½lb) Côte de Boeuf bone-in ribeye. It's showstopping, more forgiving to cook and oh-so-flavourful. Whether you're searing it over red-hot coals or pan-roasting it indoors, this method guarantees juicy, tender steak with a beautiful crust every time.

Steak Choice & Prep

Cut: Go for a large cut like Côte de Boeuf. Sharing is caring!

Seasoning: Equal parts freshly ground black pepper and Maldon salt. Optional: garlic granules.

Oil: Brush with hickory smoked rapeseed oil.

→ **Tip:** Remove the steak from the fridge 1 hour before cooking. Season and oil 30 minutes before cooking. Let it come to room temperature – this ensures even cooking.

COOKING METHOD: BBQ vs. Kitchen

1. BBQ METHOD (recommended!)

Setup: Two-zone cooking – coals on one side, none on the other (or burners on/off for gas barbecue).
Sear: Place the steak directly over hot coals. Close the lid and set a timer for 2 minutes. Flip, then repeat for another 2 minutes.
Crust check: Check the sear. If needed, sear the edges by holding the steak with tongs for 20–30 seconds.
Indirect cook: Move to the cooler side, the bone side facing the coals, if bone-in.
Target temperature: Remove the steak at 52°C (125°F) internal for medium-rare, rest to 55°C (131°F).

2. INDOOR METHOD

Preheat: Heat the oven to 180°C/160°C fan (350°F) and a cast-iron pan until smoking hot.
Sear: Sear the steak in the pan, turning every minute and cooking for 2–3 minutes total.
Flavour boost: Add butter, thyme and smashed garlic. Baste generously.
Roast: Transfer to the oven until the internal temperature reaches 52°C (125°F).

RESTING AND SLICING

Whichever cooking method you use, transfer the steak to a wire rack and tent loosely with foil. Rest for one-third of the total cook time. Why the wire rack? This keeps the crust crispy on both sides of the steak by elevating the meat and avoiding the juices moistening the crust. Always cut across the grain for maximum tenderness.

DONENESS GUIDE (internal temperatures)

→ **RARE:** 45–50°C (113–122°F)
→ **MEDIUM RARE:** 55–60°C (131–140°F)
→ **MEDIUM:** 60–65°C (140–149°F)
→ **MEDIUM WELL DONE:** 65–70°C (149–158°F)
→ **WELL DONE:** 70°C+ (158°F+)

FLAME-GRILLED BURGERS

The ultimate backyard bite

 **Prep Time:** 20 minutes

 **Cook Time:** 30 minutes

SERVES 4

4 burger patties

4 burger buns, sliced in half

Mayonnaise, for spreading

Sea salt and freshly ground black pepper

Big heat, simple moves, huge payoff. This flame-grilled burger runs a juicy, well-seasoned patty over hot grates for smoky edges and a clean melt. Stack on a soft toasted bun with crisp lettuce, sharp pickles and BBQ cider caramelised onions or fire-roasted tomato and pepper relish – or both – for the definitive crowd-pleaser on any outdoor spread.

Prep
Season the patties generously with salt and pepper just before grilling.

Charcoal: Using natural charcoal, light your coals and set up for two-zone cooking, one side with coals for high heat (230–290°C/ 450–550°F), one cooler side for finishing and cooking through.

Gas BBQ: Preheat on high with the lid down for 10–15 minutes, keeping a zone without any direct heat. e.g. 2 burners on and 1–2 burners off. The grill should be screaming hot – you want a good sear.

Grill
Place the patties on the hot side of the grill. Grill for 3–4 minutes per side. Avoid pressing the patties down as this squeezes out the juices.

Once the exterior sear is achieved, move the burgers to the cooler side to finish cooking so you don't burn the exterior.

The burgers are cooked when the internal temperature reaches 57°C (134°F) for medium rare, 63°C (145°F) for medium and 71°C (159°F) for well done.

Want cheese? Add a slice during the last minute of cooking, and close the lid to help it melt.

Toast the bun halves on the grill – this helps the buns keep their form – before adding the other ingredients. Smear a little mayonnaise over the buns, then grill, cut-side down, for 30–60 seconds until golden and crisp.

Serve
Remove and rest the burgers off the heat for 2–3 minutes to let the juices redistribute. Load up the burger buns with the burgers and any other ingredients you like to add.

BBQ CIDER CARAMELISED ONIONS

Rich, tangy and just the right amount of sweet

Prep Time: 5 minutes

Cook Time: 25–30 minutes

SERVES 4

- 2 rashers of smoked Finnebrogue bacon
- 2 onions, thinly sliced
- Pinch of sea salt
- 1 tbsp olive oil (optional)
- 100ml (3½fl oz) Magners Irish Cider
- 1 tbsp soft brown sugar
- 1 tbsp apple cider vinegar

These cider-glazed onions are a killer topping for barbecue burgers, hotdogs or anything coming off the grill. They also elevate a grilled cheese toastie like nothing else. Using Magners Irish Cider brings an extra-crisp apple note that pairs beautifully with smoky meats.

Prep

Dice and crisp up the bacon in a pan before adding the onions. It adds a smoky, salty hit that balances the sweetness and turns this into a next-level burger topping.

Sweat the onions over a medium-low heat with a pinch of salt, cooking slowly for 15–20 minutes in the bacon fat (add a little olive oil if needed), stirring occasionally, until golden and soft.

Pour in the cider and let it simmer gently until it reduces to a syrupy glaze (5–7 minutes). Stir in the brown sugar and apple cider vinegar. Cook for a few more minutes until sticky and rich.

FIRE-ROASTED TOMATO & PEPPER RELISH

Smoky-sweet with a gentle kick

Prep Time: 15 minutes

Cook Time: 25–30 minutes

- 4 ripe tomatoes
- 2 red peppers
- 1 red chilli
- 2 tbsp olive oil
- 1 small red onion, finely diced
- 2 garlic cloves, minced
- 1 tbsp soft brown sugar
- 2 tbsp red wine vinegar or apple cider vinegar
- Pinch of smoked paprika or a splash of Worcestershire sauce (optional, for depth)
- Sea salt and freshly ground black pepper

This relish turns blistered tomatoes and charred peppers into a spreadable upgrade for any BBQ, or even a cheeky cheese toastie. Batch it once, stash it in the fridge and put it on everything fresh off the grill.

Think smoky salsa meets summer jam: charred tomatoes and peppers blitzed into a bright, slightly fiery relish. It's the jar I reach for when wanting something that's sweet, tangy and with just enough heat to wake up anything it touches. Spoon it over burgers and grilled sausages, pile onto halloumi or BBQ chicken, or tuck it into a gooey cheese toastie. It also doubles as a quick cheat: swirl through mayo for a burger sauce, mix with yoghurt for a dip, fold into warm grains or beans or use it to glaze roast veg and chops right before serving... The options are endless.

Prep

Preheat the BBQ to a medium-high heat (180–230°C/350–450°F). Place the tomatoes, peppers and chilli directly on the barbecue over the hot coals until the skins are blistered and charred. Turn occasionally for even roasting, about 10–12 minutes.

Transfer the charred veg to a bowl and cover with cling film or a lid. Let them steam for 5–10 minutes – this loosens the skins. Once cool enough to handle, peel off the charred skins (no need to be perfect), then chop the flesh finely, discarding cores and most seeds.

In a pan, heat the olive oil over a medium heat. Add the diced red onion and garlic. Sauté until softened and fragrant, about 5 minutes. Add the chopped roasted tomatoes, peppers and chilli to the pan. Stir in the sugar, vinegar and a pinch of salt and pepper. Simmer gently for 15–20 minutes, stirring occasionally, until thick and jammy. Adjust the seasoning to taste and add the smoked paprika or Worcestershire sauce if desired.

Serve

Let it cool slightly before serving. This keeps well in the fridge for up to a week.

→ **Add A Kick:** Add fresh chopped basil or thyme just at the very end for an additional herbaceous kick.

TEXAS-INSPIRED SMOKED BRISKET

Low and slow, the Lone Star way

Prep Time: 30 minutes, plus 1 hour resting

Cook Time: 8–10 hours

Feed a Crowd

SERVES 12–15

1 whole packer (flat and point) brisket (around 5–6kg/11–13lb)

Signature brisket rub (see page 226) or sea salt and freshly ground black pepper

480–720ml (16–25fl oz) beef stock or bone broth

When you're cooking brisket the Texas way, you're chasing two things: a deep, smoky bark and that signature melt-in-your-mouth tenderness. This recipe walks the line between tradition and flexibility, with room to cook it on your terms – just don't rush it.

Brisket isn't done when the clock says it's done – it's ready when it jiggles like a big ol' barbecue marshmallow and probes like room-temperature butter. Serve with classic sides like pickles and sliced white bread.

Prep

Prepping a brisket is where your cook really starts. Get this right, and the rest falls into place. The goal? Create a brisket that's shaped to cook evenly, develop great bark and hold up beautifully over a long smoke.

Start cold – seriously cold! Trimming is much easier when the brisket is firm, so if you've just pulled it from the fridge, consider popping it into the freezer for 30–45 minutes. That'll firm up the fat and make everything more manageable. And don't skimp on your tools here – a razor-sharp knife is essential for clean, confident cuts.

First up, streamline the shape. Briskets aren't known for their natural aerodynamics, but trimming off any sharp corners or square edges will help the heat and smoke flow evenly over the surface. You want it smooth and rounded, not boxy – those corners just dry out anyway.

Flip to the fat cap and trim it down to a consistent 8mm (⅓in) thickness. Remove the portion of meat sticking up on top, known as the mohawk; tempting as it is to leave it, you'll get a better cooking experience and finished product by removing it. You're looking for balance – enough to baste the meat as it cooks, but not so much that it blocks the bark. Cut away any heavy deposits of dense, waxy fat – especially that wedge of fat between the point and flat as it never renders and will just get in the way of good eating. Trimming it on the point (or fatty end) will remove the exterior fat cap, so season the meat under this portion then leave the fat cap on to protect the flat portion during the cook. Generally, I find the point end has enough intermuscular fat to sustain it without the need for the exterior fat cap. Every pitmaster will have their own views and way of trimming the brisket.

On the meat side, remove any silver skin or webbing that's hiding the grain. Exposing that muscle fibre will help your rub cling properly and give the smoke a direct path to the meat. Don't throw away the trimmings – brisket offcuts are full of potential.

Mince them for burger patties or render down for tallow. It's all good eating if you treat it right.

Once trimmed, coat the brisket in a simple rub of coarse salt and freshly ground black pepper, 50/50, or alternatively my signature brisket rub! Apply it from a bit of height for an even layer, making sure to hit the sides as well. Treat the brisket like a roast, not just a slab – every surface needs seasoning.

After that, stash it in the fridge, uncovered. That gives the seasoning time to sink in and helps form a dry surface, which is key to developing a serious bark once it hits the smoker.

Grill
Begin with the bark building phase. Set up your smoker for indirect heat at around 120°C (248°F) using your favourite hardwood (oak is the Texas classic). Trim any excess fat from the brisket, leaving a 5mm (¼in) cap on top. I tend to leave more fat on the flat as the point already has a good amount of intermuscular fat. Remove the mohawk from the brisket, if still attached, and trim the edges so the flat end is at least 4cm (1½in) thick. Make sure to round off the edges.

Season generously with salt and pepper or your go-to beef rub. Place the brisket fat-side up (or down, depending on your smoker) and smoke, unwrapped, until a dark bark forms and the meat stops absorbing smoke – this usually takes 4–5 hours. Cooking time will vary depending on your brisket's size, marbling and even the breed of cattle. Trust your eyes, your hands and your thermometer.

If you notice liquid pooling on your brisket, place a small chunk of wood wrapped in foil under this area to allow the liquid to drain away. You want to avoid any pools of liquid which will impact the bark building. The meat is ready for the next stage when the bark turns a deep mahogany colour and has a dry, textured surface, but also an internal temperature of 65–70°C (149–158°F) in the thickest part.

When you hit those markers, it's time to use the 'Texas Crutch' method – wrapping the brisket tightly in foil or butcher paper to trap heat and moisture and speed up the cook. It is also possible to cook using a foil boat, which basically means the bark on top remains exposed, but you slowly braise the brisket in its own juices from underneath. Alternatively, it's possible to cook the entire way through without using any wrap or crutch.

When wrapping, you can use tin foil or butcher's paper. Use foil to create a snug boat for the brisket. I find it best to use 3–4 layers of foil on top of each other to create added strength, especially as you will likely be moving the brisket around during this next stage.

Spray the butcher paper with water to make it more pliable for wrapping then place the brisket in the dampened butcher paper or foil. Add some melted beef tallow or beef broth – not too much, just enough to keep it moist, about 120ml (4fl oz). Wrap tightly with foil or paper to trap the steam and juices, then transfer the brisket to a large, heavy-duty foil roasting tray, fat-side down. This will aid in moving the brisket around.

Return the brisket (in the tray) to the smoker. Continue cooking for another 4–5 hours, checking every hour or

so. You'll know it's done when it feels soft and jiggly when pressed through the foil (like a giant marshmallow) and the internal temperature is 90–96°C (194–205°F). However, tenderness is the true test: the probe should glide into the brisket without effort. Similar to probing a block of room-temperature butter.

Carefully transfer the covered brisket to a dry, insulated cooler. Close the lid and let it rest for at least 1 hour – do not skip this stage. This allows the juices to redistribute and the muscle fibres to fully relax. This can also be done by wrapping it in a towel and leaving it in the kitchen or someplace warm. At this stage we want the internal temperature of the brisket to reduce to 65°C (149°F) before slicing.

Serve

Remove the brisket from the tray and transfer it to a cutting board, saving all the meat juices in the tray. If the colour isn't quite dark enough for your liking, let the brisket sit out of the foil for a couple of minutes – oxygen will help darken the bark a little.

Slice against the grain into pencil-thin strips, then dip each slice in the reserved juices and serve with any remaining sauce poured over the top.

RED WINE BRAISED SHORT RIBS

Meltingly tender short ribs braised low and slow

 Prep Time: 20 minutes

 Cook Time: 2½–8 hours (depending on method)

SERVES 4–6

- 2.25kg (5lb) bone-in beef short ribs
- Fine pink Himalayan salt and freshly ground black pepper
- 1 yellow onion, thinly sliced
- 2 shallots, thinly sliced
- 1 head garlic, halved crosswise (skin on)
- 480ml (16fl oz) dry red wine (like Cabernet Sauvignon)
- 480ml (16fl oz) low-sodium beef broth
- 2 tbsp tomato paste
- 4 sprigs of fresh thyme, plus extra to garnish
- 2 sprigs of fresh rosemary
- 2 bay leaves

When the air starts to cool and the leaves begin to fall, this dish hits the spot like no other. It's our go-to whenever we want a comforting, rich meal without the fuss. The magic? A deep red wine braise that transforms humble short ribs into something seriously indulgent. This version is flexible – whether you're around the firepit, slow-cooking in the kitchen or letting the barbecue do its thing, these ribs bring serious depth and warmth. Serve it up with the buttery, whipped, creamy potatoes (trust us, it's a game changer), and you've got a rib-sticking meal you'll crave year-round.

COOKING OPTIONS

BBQ / Kamado Style (Indirect Heat, 160–180°C/325–350°F):
Season the short ribs with approx. 2 teaspoons each of salt and pepper 5–10 minutes before searing them over direct heat in a cast-iron pan or Dutch oven until browned (3–5 minutes per side). Add the onion, shallots, garlic, wine, broth, tomato paste and herbs. Cover with foil or a lid. Move to indirect heat, close the lid, and cook for 3 hours until the ribs are fall-apart tender.

Campfire:
Season the short ribs with approx. 2 teaspoons each of salt and pepper 5–10 minutes before searing and braising everything in a Dutch oven over glowing coals. Nestle the pot into the firepit and rotate every 30 minutes. Add coals as needed to maintain a low simmer for 3–3½ hours.

Kitchen / Oven:
Preheat the oven to 160°C/140°C fan (325°F). Sear the ribs, sauté the onion and shallots, then return the ribs to the pot with the remaining ingredients. Cover and roast for 2½–3 hours in the oven until tender.

Slow Cooker:
Sear the ribs and sauté the aromatics in a pan first. Transfer everything to the slow cooker and cook on LOW for 8 hours or HIGH for 4–5 hours.

Serve
Plate a big scoop of creamy buttery mash, top with a couple of ribs and spoon over that rich red wine sauce. Finish with a sprinkle of fresh thyme.

➔ `Quick Bourbon-Braised Short Ribs: Swap the red wine for 370ml (13fl oz) bourbon and 120ml (4fl oz) beef broth. Keep everything else the same - onion, shallots, garlic, tomato paste and herbs.`

➔ `Bonus Bourbon Boost: Stir 2 extra tablespoons of bourbon into the braising liquid during the last 15 minutes of cooking for a deeper, more pronounced flavour.`

TEXAS-STYLE BEEF CHILLI

Rich, bold and, just like a great BBQ, full of warmth and character

 Prep Time: 25 minutes

 Cook Time: 1½ hours

SERVES 6–8

- 1kg (2¼lb) beef brisket or rump steak, trimmed and sliced into 2.5cm (1in) thick pieces across the grain
- 6 rashers of smoked bacon, chopped
- 1 yellow onion, sliced
- 1 red onion, sliced
- 2 red peppers, deseeded and diced
- 2 garlic cloves, minced
- 1 heaped tsp hot chilli powder (or 1 level tbsp if using mild, adjust for heat)
- 1 tsp smoked paprika
- 1 tsp ground cumin
- 500g (17oz) minced beef
- ½ tsp dried oregano
- 1 tbsp tomato purée
- 1 beef stock cube (optional, if not using smoked brisket)
- 2 × 400g (14oz) tins of chopped tomatoes
- 240ml (8fl oz) fresh coffee (optional, highly recommended)
- 2 tsp dark chocolate, grated, or cocoa powder (optional)
- Sea salt and freshly ground black pepper

Over the last few years, my visits to Texas have deepened my love for true barbecue and, of course, Texas chilli. What sets Texas chilli apart? It's all about the beef – no beans, just rich, smoky, hearty chunks of meat that simmer to perfection. During my travels through the Lone Star State, I was lucky enough to witness the kind of slow-cooked magic that makes every Texan chilli unique, where layers of flavour develop over time with a deep, smoky profile and a bit of heat. This recipe takes that inspiration and brings it home with a combination of minced beef, tender leftover brisket and the addition of smoked bacon and spices to create the kind of chilli you'll want to ladle onto everything – from baked potatoes to fresh flatbreads – or just serve in a bowl with nachos for dipping.

Prep

Season the brisket or rump steak with salt and pepper, and seal the meat in a hot pan. Set aside. If you're looking for that true Texas smokiness, you can smoke the brisket or rump for 3–4 hours before adding it to the chilli.

In a Dutch oven or large pot, add the chopped bacon and cook until it begins to brown. Toss in the onions, peppers, garlic and spices, along with the minced beef, and cook until browned.

Add the brisket (or rump) to the pot with all the other ingredients and stir to combine. When pouring in the tinned tomatoes, add half a tin of water or a cup of fresh coffee for a deeper flavour. Let everything simmer until it starts bubbling, then cover with a lid.

Set the barbecue to 180°C (350°F) or the oven at 180°C/160°C fan (350°F).

Grill

Transfer to the oven or barbecue for 1 hour, stirring occasionally.

If you like, about 30 minutes in, add some grated dark chocolate or cocoa powder for extra richness and complexity.

→ **Add Some Heat:** Adjust the chilli powder level or add a few fresh diced jalapeños for that extra Texan kick.
→ **Sweet and Savoury:** Add a dollop of soured cream or a sprinkle of Cheddar cheese when serving, for extra richness.

BEEF ROAST *with* CAJUN-SPICED POTATO CAKES

Southern-spiced backyard BBQ meets classic Sunday roast

 Prep Time: 30 minutes

 Cook Time: 1½ hours, plus resting

SERVES 6–8

2–3kg (4½–6½lb) 2-bone rib of beef
2 tsp crushed garlic
1 tsp chopped fresh rosemary
285g (9½oz) Fiery Fresh Salsa (page 238)
Sea salt and freshly ground black pepper

FOR THE CAJUN-SPICED POTATO CAKES

4 medium potatoes, boiled in their jackets
2 eggs, lightly beaten
2 tsp Cajun seasoning
2 tbsp plain flour, plus extra for dusting
½ tsp salt
2 tbsp olive oil

This one's a mash-up that came to life after a road trip through the American South. Somewhere between a smoky Texas brisket and a back-porch dinner in Louisiana, I had a roast beef sandwich with spicy potato hash on the side, and I couldn't stop thinking about it. Back home, I gave it my own barbecue twist. A juicy standing rib roast cooked low and slow on the grill, paired with crispy Cajun-spiced potato cakes and a spoonful of our Fiery Fresh Salsa (page 238) to tie it all together. It's an easy showstopper. The Cajun cakes bring the heat and crunch, while the salsa keeps it fresh. Serve it family-style and let everyone dive in. It's comfort food with a spicy twist – straight from the grill to the soul.

Prep

Rub the beef with salt, pepper, the garlic and chopped rosemary. Let it rest at room temperature for 20 minutes. Keep your salsa ready in a small saucepan.

For ceramic or kettle barbecues: set up for indirect medium-high heat (180–230°C/350–450°F).

Grill

Place the roast over a drip tray, cover and cook for 1–1½ hours, or until the internal temperature hits 51°C (123°F). Remove from the grill and rest under foil for 20 minutes before carving.

Peel and mash the boiled potatoes in a large bowl. Stir in the eggs, Cajun seasoning, flour and salt. Shape into 16 patties with floured hands. Cook on an oiled barbecue plate or grill for about 5 minutes per side until golden.

Serve

Heat the salsa while the potato cakes cook. Slice the beef, plate it up with the Cajun cakes, and spoon over the warm salsa.

➔ **Mash Up:** Try sweet potatoes or mash in roasted corn for extra flavour.
➔ **Spice It Up:** Swap the salsa for smoky BBQ sauce or a chimichurri (see pages 234 or 235).
➔ **Add A Kick:** Add chopped chillies, green onions or cheese into the potato cakes for extra kick.
➔ **No Waste:** Any leftover beef makes epic sandwiches the next day.

PITMASTER'S PASTA PIE

Cheesy baked rigatoni you can slice like a lasagne-cake

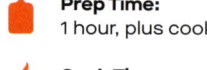
Prep Time: 1 hour, plus cooling

Cook Time: 2½ hours

SERVES 6–8

FOR THE BEEF RAGÙ

2 tbsp olive oil
1 large onion, diced
4 garlic cloves, finely chopped
500g (17oz) minced beef
2 × 400g (14oz) tins of chopped tomatoes
100g (3½oz) tomato paste
2 bay leaves
250ml (9fl oz) red wine
Sea salt and freshly ground black pepper

FOR THE PASTA ASSEMBLY

750g (1lb 11oz) rigatoni pasta
Olive oil, to drizzle
600ml (1 pint) béchamel sauce (see page 186)
70g (3oz) Cheddar, grated
60g (2½oz) Parmesan, finely grated
Handful of fresh parsley, roughly chopped

This is the kind of dish that stops a BBQ dead in its tracks; a towering, golden-crusted rigatoni pasta pie packed with slow-cooked beef ragù, creamy béchamel sauce and bubbling cheese. Inspired by the Italian classic timballo, we've given it a barbecue spin that makes it perfect for your smoker or grill with indirect heat. It's built for the kind of gathering where people hover around the pit with cold drinks and big appetites.

Make the ragù a day in advance if you want to get ahead – the flavour only gets better through resting – then take your time assembling the pie. The result is dramatic, rich and absolutely built to impress. Serve it straight from the grill with a cold beer or glass of wine and some fresh herbs scattered over the top.

Prep

In a large pan, heat the olive oil over a medium-low heat. Sauté the onion for 3 minutes, then add the garlic and cook for another minute. Turn the heat up to medium-high, add the beef and cook for 10 minutes, breaking it up with a wooden spoon, until browned. Stir in the tomatoes, tomato paste, bay leaves and red wine. Bring to the boil, then reduce to a simmer and cook, partially covered, for 1½ hours until thickened. Season to taste. (The ragù can be made a day ahead and stored in the fridge.)

When ready to assemble, bring a large pot of salted water to a rolling boil. Add the rigatoni and cook for about 5 minutes – until just shy of al dente. Drain, tip back into the pan and drizzle with olive oil, then toss to prevent sticking.

Preheat the barbecue to 200°C (400°F), set up for indirect cooking. Set a 22cm (8¾in) springform cake tin onto a round, cast-iron skillet. Spread a thick layer of béchamel over the base of the tin, then smear some béchamel on one side of each rigatoni and stand them vertically, side by side, packed tightly. Carefully spoon the ragù over the pasta, letting it fill each tube. Press down gently to compact the ragù. Sprinkle the grated cheeses evenly over the top.

Bake

Bake on the barbecue for 30–45 minutes until bubbling and golden on top. Rest for 10 minutes before releasing the ring.

Serve

Garnish with chopped parsley and slice like a cake. Serve with a crisp salad or extra béchamel on the side.

→ **Cheese Swap:** Try mozzarella, fontina or provolone for extra cheesy stretch.

→ **Meaty Twist:** Add chopped pancetta or Italian sausage to the ragù.

BÉCHAMEL SAUCE

MAKES ABOUT 600ML (1 PINT)

 Prep Time: 5 minutes

 Cook Time: 10–12 minutes

80g (3oz) unsalted butter
50g (2oz) plain flour
500ml (17fl oz) whole milk
Sea salt, to taste
Freshly grated nutmeg, to taste

Prep
Set a saucepan over a medium heat and melt the butter until it starts to foam. Stir in the flour and cook it out for a couple of minutes, whisking gently, it should start to smell a little nutty and turn a light golden shade.

Pour in half the milk in a slow stream, whisking all the time until the mixture is smooth and starts to thicken slightly. Gradually add the rest of the milk, keeping the whisk moving to avoid lumps. Once fully combined, switch to a wooden spoon. Let the sauce gently bubble for around 5 minutes, stirring often until it thickens and coats the back of a spoon.

Serve
Season with sea salt and a generous pinch of grated nutmeg. Take it off the heat and keep covered until ready to use.

→ **Make It Cheesy:** Add in a handful of grated mature Cheddar or smoked cheese to turn this into a quick white cheese sauce.
→ **Bring in the BBQ Flavours:** Stir in a spoonful of mustard or BBQ rub to tie it back into the grill.

SMOKY SLOW-COOKED BEEF SHARING PLATTER

A BBQ built for a crowd

 Prep Time: 30 minutes

 Cook Time: 4–5 hours, plus 2 hours smoking (optional)

 Feeds a Crowd

SERVES 6–8

- 3.5kg (8lb) beef shin, cut into large chunks or split for faster cooking
- 3 tbsp neutral oil (such as rapeseed or avocado oil)
- 3 tbsp steak seasoning (such as Sucklebusters Campfire or your own blend)
- 4 white onions, diced
- 8 garlic cloves, finely chopped
- 3 tbsp ground cumin
- 3 tbsp dried oregano
- 600ml (1 pint) beer (such as Birra Moretti or any pale lager)
- 500ml (17fl oz) beef stock
- 400g (14oz) tin of chipotle peppers in adobo sauce
- 60ml (2½fl oz) fresh lime juice
- 6 tbsp apple cider vinegar
- 5 tsp sea salt
- 3 tsp freshly ground black pepper
- ¼ tsp ground cloves
- 6 bay leaves

TO SERVE (optional)

- Mexican rice or dirty rice
- Warmed flour tortillas
- Smashed or sliced avocado
- Pico de gallo
- Crinkle-cut chips or fries
- Melted cheese or crumbly queso fresco

When you're cooking for a party, you want something that's big on flavour, easy to prep ahead and made for piling high on platters. This slow-cooked beef dish ticks every box. It's smoky, tender and packed with rich, spicy depth, perfect for loading into warm tortillas with all your favourite toppings. Serve it up with a mix of fresh salsas, avocado, cheese and rice, and let everyone build their own plate. It's the kind of hands-on, flavour-packed feast that brings people together and keeps them coming back for more.

Prep

If using a smoker or barbecue, get it running at 110°C (230°F) indirect heat.

Lightly coat the beef with oil and season generously with your steak rub.

Grill

Smoke until the bark forms and the surface is dry to the touch, about 2 hours. This adds extra depth, but if skipping the smoke, just grill or sear the beef until browned all over.

In a heavy-based pot or cast-iron Dutch oven, heat a splash of oil over a medium-high heat. Once hot, add the smoked or seared beef and brown it on all sides, working in batches if needed. Set aside.

In the same pot, add the onions and cook until softened. Stir in the garlic, cumin and oregano, letting everything bloom for a minute or two. Pour in the beer, beef stock, chipotle with sauce, lime juice, vinegar, salt, pepper, ground cloves and bay leaves. Give it a stir and bring to a gentle boil.

Nestle the beef into the broth, reduce to a low simmer, and cover.

Let it bubble gently for 3–4 hours, topping up with more stock or beer as needed. Once the meat pulls apart with a fork, you're there.

Serve

Remove and discard the bay leaves. Shred the beef in the pot to soak up all that smoky, spicy broth. Transfer to a large platter and serve it up hot, with rice, tortillas, avocado, chips and cheese.

→ `Made for Sharing:` Let guests build their own – load it into tacos, roll up burritos, or scoop it with chips. The braising liquor also doubles as a banging birria-style dip.

CRISPY CHILLI BEEF

That cheeky fakeaway night that hits better than your go-to takeaway

Prep Time: 20 minutes, plus 15–30 minutes marinating

Cook Time: 20 minutes

Equipment: Wok

SERVES 4

- 2 sirloin steaks, thinly sliced into matchstick-like strips
- 1 egg, beaten
- 100g (3½oz) cornflour
- Vegetable oil, for shallow-frying
- 1 small onion, sliced
- 1 small red pepper, sliced
- 2–3 spring onions, sliced
- 1 fresh red chilli, finely chopped

FOR THE MARINADE
- 1 tbsp light soy sauce
- 3 garlic cloves, minced
- ½ tsp grated ginger (jarred is totally fine)
- 1 tsp sesame oil
- ½ tsp white sugar
- ¼ tsp white pepper

FOR THE STIR-FRY SAUCE
- 3 tbsp sweet chilli sauce
- 2 tbsp ketchup
- 2 tbsp light soy sauce
- 1 tsp white or rice vinegar
- 1 tbsp sugar
- ½ tsp salt

TO SERVE (optional)
- Steamed jasmine rice
- Stir-fried egg noodles
- Wraps

This dish was born from a craving – one of those 'I want something crispy, sticky, spicy… but I want it now' kinda cravings. And wow, does this one deliver. Thin strips of steak, fried until golden and crunchy, tossed in a sweet-spicy-sticky glaze that coats every bite like a dream. It's fast, it's fiery and it's freakishly addictive. Whether you serve it up with noodles, fluffy rice or stuff it in a wrap for a next-level lunch, this is one of those recipes you'll go back to again and again. I promise it'll never make it to leftovers.

Prep
Whisk together your marinade ingredients, toss in the beef, and set aside to soak up all that flavour for 15–30 minutes.

In a small bowl, combine all the stir-fry sauce ingredients. This sauce is your sticky, spicy magic – set it aside until you're ready to stir-fry.

Once the beef has marinated, mix the egg into the beef mix, then remove the strips and toss in a bowl with the cornflour to coat well. Make sure they're fully dusted but not clumped together – shake off any excess.

Heat about 5cm (2in) of oil in a wok or deep pan to 190°C (375°F).

Grill
Fry the beef in small batches for 1–2 minutes until golden, crispy and glorious. Don't overcrowd the pan when frying – give those beef strips space to crisp up properly. You want sizzle, not steam! Drain on kitchen paper or a wire rack.

Wipe out your wok, add a touch of oil, and throw in the sliced onion and red pepper. Stir for a minute or two until softened.

Add your crispy beef to the wok along with the stir-fry sauce. Toss everything together over a high heat until the beef is beautifully coated and sticky. Add the spring onions and chilli for that final punch.

Serve
Pile it high on a plate and dive in immediately. Serve with steamed jasmine rice and stir-fried egg noodles, or roll it into wraps for a spicy street-food-style vibe.

BBQ wok setup:
Use something like the Weber GBS / Kamado Joe accessory ring

If you're going full barbecue mode, this dish shines on a wok over live fire using the Weber Gourmet BBQ System or a Kamado Joe wok ring. Here's how to nail it:

Gear Needed:
- Carbon-steel or cast-iron wok
- GBS wok insert or Kamado Joe wok ring
- Long-handled tongs/spatula
- Heat-resistant gloves

Setup Tips:
Build a hot fire – lumpwood charcoal works best. You want strong, direct heat under the wok.

Place the wok in the ring and let it preheat until it's smoking hot (this only takes a few minutes).

Add your oil and quickly fry the beef strips in batches – be quick, as high heat = fast cook.

Stir-fry the veg and toss everything together right there over the fire. You'll get a touch of smoky wok hei (that charred magic) that's tough to get indoors with the heat constraints of a home kitchen.

➜ **Pro Tip:** Have all your ingredients prepped and ready before you start cooking – this is fast and furious wok cooking at its best.

PHILLY CHEESE STEAK TEAR & SHARE WHEEL

The ultimate BBQ sharing snack

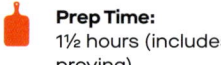
Prep Time: 1½ hours (includes proving)

Cook Time: 20 minutes

SERVES 6–8

FOR THE DOUGH (makes 2 bases)

730g (1lb 10oz) bread flour
450ml (15fl oz) warm water (150ml/5fl oz boiled + 300ml/10fl oz tap, around 32–35°C/90–95°F)
18g (¾oz) salt
7g (1 packet) instant dried yeast

FOR THE FILLING

3 onions, sliced
1 red pepper, sliced
1 green pepper, sliced
Oil, for frying
2 sirloin steaks
165g (5½oz) cream cheese
115–230g (4–8oz) mozzarella, grated
115–230g (4–8oz) Cheddar, grated
1 egg yolk, for brushing

FOR THE CHEESE SAUCE

250ml (9fl oz) double cream
½ tsp chilli powder
¼ tsp garlic powder or granules
¼ tsp cayenne pepper
¼ tsp paprika
2 tsp cornflour
100g (3½oz) Cheddar, grated
100g (3½oz) Red Leicester or Mexican cheese, grated
Sea salt and freshly ground black pepper

There are barbecue snacks... and then there's this. It's that golden, melty, crispy-edged crowd-pleaser that you throw on the table and just watch disappear. No knives. No forks. Just hands reaching in, tearing off cheesy, smoky, irresistible bites straight from the board. It's simple, satisfying and made to be shared. Serve with a bowl of that cheesy dipping sauce on the side, some pickles and a few ice-cold beers. It's Philly meets pizza night. And it's a guaranteed hit.

We threw this one together during a relaxing evening barbecue with neighbours – music on, smoke in the air and not a single bite left by the end of the night. It's the kind of snack that feels like summer.

Prep
Combine all the dough ingredients in a large bowl and knead until smooth (about 10 minutes by hand or 5 in a mixer). Cover with a damp cloth and let it prove until doubled in size – roughly an hour, depending on the room temperature.

Once your dough has proved, divide and roll one ball into a 25–30cm (10–12in) round – the other can be kept in the fridge for 4–5 days or frozen for future use. Use a pizza cutter to slice a small cross or X in the centre (this will help form the tear and share effect later).

Sauté the onions and peppers in a bit of oil until softened and caramelised. Set aside.

For the cheese sauce, in a small pan, heat your cream over a medium-low heat. Whisk in the spices and cornflour until smooth and thickened. Add the grated cheeses and stir until melted and velvety. Season to taste. Preheat the grill to high (230°C/450°F).

Grill
Season your sirloins well and grill to your preferred temperature. We pulled ours off at 54°C (130°F) or medium rare. Rest and slice thinly.

Spread a ring of cream cheese around the outer third of the dough. Layer the sliced steak, sautéed veg, mozzarella and Cheddar over the cream cheese. Take each inner triangle of dough that you have sliced from the centre and fold it outwards and over the filling, tucking it underneath the dough ring to seal in the filling. This creates that classic wheel look.

Brush the dough with egg yolk for a glossy golden crust. Bake at 225°C (430°F) indirect (oven or barbecue) until golden and cooked through – roughly 15–20 minutes.

Serve
Serve the steak wheel immediately, with the warm cheese sauce for dipping or drizzling, if you like.

SESAME-SOY BEEF KEBABS with HOMEMADE FLATBREADS

A backyard BBQ classic with a twist

Prep Time: 25 minutes, plus 4 hours marinating

Cook Time: 20 minutes

Equipment: Metal or bamboo skewers (bamboo soaked for 30 minutes)

SERVES 4–6

- 700–900g (1lb 9oz–2lb) rump or sirloin steak, cut into 4cm (1½in) cubes
- Vegetables of choice (such as peppers, red onion, courgettes)
- Salad, to serve

FOR THE MARINADE
- 150ml (5fl oz) soy sauce
- 60ml (2½fl oz) sesame oil
- 120ml (4fl oz) vegetable oil
- 6 garlic cloves, minced
- 1 tbsp grated fresh ginger
- 2 tbsp sesame seeds
- 4 tbsp sugar
- ¼ tsp black pepper

FOR THE FLATBREADS
- 240ml (8fl oz) Greek yoghurt
- 125g (4½oz) self-raising flour
- Pinch of salt
- Melted butter, for brushing

This one came together during a sunny afternoon when I wanted something bold and flavour-packed but still easy to share. I had a few steaks on hand, some veggies in the fridge and a craving for something with that sweet-salty umami punch. A quick sesame-soy marinade, some homemade flatbreads, and we were off. It's now one of my go-to barbecue meals for when friends are over, and I want maximum flavour with minimal fuss. Smoky, savoury and seriously satisfying, paired with the soft, warm flatbreads and some crisp salad, it's a feast made for fire and friends. It's casual, hands-on food that brings everyone to the table.

Prep

Combine all the marinade ingredients in a jar and shake well. Pour this over the steak cubes in a bowl or bag, mix and marinate in the fridge for 4 hours.

Mix the Greek yoghurt, flour and salt in a bowl until it forms a dough. Let it rest for 10 minutes.

Thread the marinated beef and vegetables onto skewers, alternating pieces for even cooking.

Preheat the barbecue to medium-high (180–230°C/350–450°F).

Grill

Grill the kebabs for 8–10 minutes, turning occasionally, until caramelised and cooked to your liking.

Roll the flatbread dough into 4 rounds about 5mm (¼in) thick. Cook on a hot, dry pan or directly over the grill for about 1–2 minutes on each side.

Serve

Brush the flatbreads with melted butter once off the heat. Plate up the kebabs with salad and warm flatbreads. Let everyone build their own wraps or enjoy it all separately.

→ **Citrus Kick:** Add a splash of rice vinegar or lime juice to the marinade for extra zing.

→ **Mix Up the Meats:** Try it with lamb or chicken for a tasty variation.

→ **Add Some Flavour:** Stir some garlic and herbs into the flatbread dough for extra flavour.

→ **Spice It Up:** Serve with a dollop of chilli sauce or pickled veg on the side for contrast.

SMOKED BEEF BRISKET RAGÙ

Campfire comfort with an Italian soul

Prep Time: 20 minutes

Cook Time: 1½–2½ hours

SERVES 6

- 3 tbsp rapeseed oil
- 700g (1lb 9oz) smoked brisket (or substitute with seared rump steak)
- 2 onions, diced
- 2 carrots, diced
- 2 celery sticks, diced
- 3 garlic cloves, minced
- 2 tbsp tomato paste
- 1 tbsp plain flour
- 250ml (9fl oz) red wine
- 2 × 400g (14oz) tins of chopped tomatoes
- 500ml (17fl oz) beef broth
- A few fresh thyme sprigs or 1 tsp dried thyme
- Sea salt and freshly ground black pepper
- Fresh pasta, to serve

This dish was born out of leftovers and a little inspiration from the back of the fridge. After a long, lazy, overnight brisket cook, we had a good chunk of brisket left and couldn't bear to let it go to waste. The next day, with a chill in the air and a bit of red wine open, a slow-cooked ragù came calling. Cooking this over fire in a cast-iron pot adds that unmistakable smokiness to the rich tomato base. The brisket practically melts into the sauce, giving you a ragù that tastes like it took all day, because it kinda did. Perfect tossed through thick ribbons of fresh pappardelle and served with a glass of bold red wine. It's rustic, hearty and made for chilly evenings, full bellies and second helpings.

Prep

Set your barbecue to 180–200°C (350–400°F) for direct heat cooking. Place a cast-iron pot directly over the fire and add the oil.

If using raw rump steak, brown it off in batches and set aside before continuing with the sauce. Add the diced onions, carrots and celery to the pot and cook until softened. Stir in the garlic and cook for another 30 seconds. Add the tomato paste and mix thoroughly. Sprinkle in the flour and stir to coat all the veggies.

Pour in the wine and cook for 1–2 minutes to reduce slightly. Add the chopped tomatoes, brisket or browned beef and beef broth. Stir in the thyme and season with salt and pepper.

Pop the lid on the pot and cook until the meat is fall-apart tender; for smoked brisket that's about 1 hour, for rump steak that's 1½–2 hours.

Serve

Toss with fresh pappardelle or your pasta of choice.

→ **Want It Smokier?** Add a few chunks of wood to the fire during cooking.

→ **No Brisket?** Leftover roast beef or even shredded lamb would work beautifully too.

→ **Serve With:** Top with grated Parmesan and a drizzle of good olive oil.

THOR'S HAMMER, with CREAMY MASH & HOT HONEY VEG

Big flavours, epic presentation

Prep Time: 45 minutes, plus 1 hour resting

Cook Time: 6–8 hours

Equipment: Cherry wood chunks for smoking

Feeds a Crowd

SERVES 6–8

1 whole beef shin, bone-in
Your favourite beef rub, or a simple 50/50 salt and pepper mix
Splash of beef stock
1 can of Guinness
Sea salt and freshly ground black pepper

FOR THE CREAMY MASHED POTATOES

900g (2lb) potatoes (floury variety like Maris Piper or Yukon Gold), peeled
120g (4oz) butter, melted
120ml (4fl oz) double cream

FOR THE ROASTED VEG

Carrots, onions, garlic (as many as needed)
Rapeseed oil
Hot honey (or regular honey and dried chilli flakes)

FOR THE GRAVY

Pan juices from the wrapped beef
Remaining wrap liquid (Guinness/beef stock)
A splash of red wine
1 tbsp redcurrant jelly

This one's a true showstopper. When I first posted this recipe it went viral on both Instagram and TikTok, with over 50 million views – it's clearly the kind of cook that turns heads at a backyard barbecue.

Known as Thor's Hammer (aka beef shin on the bone), it looks like a medieval weapon and eats like a dream. We fire it up with cherry wood for a subtle sweetness, wrap it once the bark sets and cook it until the meat's fall-apart tender. Serve with mashed potatoes, roasted veg glazed with hot honey and a rich Guinness and red wine gravy.

Prep
Trim any silver skin from the beef shin. Season generously with the rub and let sit for 1 hour. Wrap the exposed bone tip with foil to prevent charring.

Set your barbecue for indirect cooking at 130°C (266°C) with cherry wood.

Grill
Place the shin on the grill and cook for about 3 hours, or until the bark has set (test by gently scratching it – if it doesn't move, it's ready). Wrap the meat in foil with a splash of beef stock and Guinness. Continue cooking until the internal temperature hits 95°C (203°F).

Once done, rest the meat for at least an hour. Wrap it in towels and pop it in a cooler or a warm space.

Prep
Boil the peeled potatoes in a pan of salted water until soft. Drain, return to the pan and dry them out over a low heat. Mash (or rice) them, then pass through a sieve for extra smoothness.

Stir in the melted butter, then gradually stir in the cream. Season to taste.

Place the carrots, onions and garlic on a tray. Drizzle with oil and season with salt and pepper.

Roast at 200°C/180°C fan (400°F) for 30–40 minutes in the oven or on the BBQ. In the last 15 minutes, drizzle over some hot honey.

In a saucepan, combine the beef drippings, remaining Guinness/stock liquid, a splash of red wine and the redcurrant jelly. Simmer and reduce by half until glossy and rich.

Serve
Pull the meat from the bone and serve over mash with the roasted veg and gravy drizzled over everything.

➔ **Smoky Edge:** Try a coffee rub for a smoky, bitter edge to balance the richness.

➔ **Give It A Kick:** Add horseradish cream or mustard mash.

SMASH BURGERS

Juicy centres, heavy crusts, melty cheese and soft buns

Prep Time: 15 minutes

Cook Time: 10 minutes

SERVES 4

100% beef mince (70:30 meat:fat ratio) ask your butcher to grind it fresh	
BBQ rub (see pages 224–9), or sea salt and freshly ground black pepper	
Slices of your favourite cheese	

ADD-ONS

Brioche buns, sliced in half	
Mayonnaise	
Lettuce	
Tomato slices	
Crispy bacon	
Sautéed mushrooms and onions	
Burger sauce	

There's something primal and perfect about a smash burger, just pure beef, fire and technique. Born from the diners of the American Midwest, this burger style has taken on a life of its own over recent years, in backyard barbecues and food trucks around the globe.

What makes it so special? It's all in the smash. By pressing a fatty meatball onto a blazing-hot griddle you create an unbeatable crust that locks in flavour while keeping the inside tender and juicy. No fillers. No fluff. Just beef, seasoning and heat.

This recipe celebrates that simplicity but leaves plenty of room to tune into your own, from adding smoked cheese to slipping in some jalapeño jam or swapping in a spicy aioli. Whether you're cooking for a crowd or just craving a burger that bites back, this one never misses. Grab your spatula, it's time to get smashing.

Prep

Form the meat into meatballs slightly larger than a golf ball (aim for 2 per smash burger).

Heat a cast-iron pan or griddle on the BBQ grill or hob until screaming hot – 240–290°C (464–550°F).

Grill

Place a meatball on the pan and smash down flat with a sturdy spatula – you want a thin patty with a deep sear, as that's where the flavour lives. Season immediately with a BBQ rub or just salt and pepper. Don't force the flip – when it's seared properly, it'll release on its own – about 60–90 seconds.

Flip, add your favourite cheese, and cover the grill to melt.

Serve

Layer up your burger: spread mayo on the bottom brioche bun, then top with lettuce, a thick beef tomato slice, 2 cheese-covered burger patties, some bacon, mushrooms, onions and burger sauce, then top off with the lid of the brioche bun.

Enjoy hot and juicy with napkins at the ready.

➜ `Smoke It Up:` Add a touch of wood smoke by placing a small smoker box or wood chips on the grill.
➜ `Spicy Twist:` Mix chopped jalapeños into the beef or top with pickled chilli.
➜ `Double Down:` Go animal-style with grilled onions, secret sauce and a lettuce wrap.

OKLAHOMA ONION SMASH
(regional twist)

Want to take your smash game to the next level? Let's head south to El Reno, Oklahoma, where the locals have been stacking onions and smashing patties long before it was cool. The Oklahoma Onion Burger is a Depression-era creation that's simple, affordable and outrageously tasty. The idea was to stretch the meat with cheap, abundant onions, but what they ended up with was pure burger genius. It's a game changer: juicy beef, sweet onions and a bit of crisp all in one glorious bite.

Here's how to do it:
After placing your meatball on the hot griddle, pile on a generous handful of paper-thin-sliced white onions. Then smash the burger through the onions so they press into the beef and start to caramelise right on the hot surface. Let it sear – the onions will get sweet, crispy and almost melt into the meat.

Flip the whole thing once the crust forms, let the onions finish cooking underneath, then hit it with your cheese.

Serve it up just like the classic version, or go minimalist with just onion burger, cheese, bun, done. Either way, you're in for a ride.

THE TERIYAKI SMASH
(Japanese-inspired)

Umami-packed, with a sweet-savoury edge

This burger is light, flavourful and dangerously addictive.

Mix a touch of soy sauce and grated ginger into your beef before forming the patties (but just a little, we still want that crust!).

After smashing, glaze the patty with a brush of teriyaki sauce. Top with a slice of mild white cheese (mozzarella or provolone works well). Add pickled daikon, nori strips and a bit of Kewpie mayo.

Serve on a steamed or toasted milk bun (like Hokkaido-style).

THE TEX-MEX SMASH

Spicy, cheesy and bold – just like Texas itself

Season your beef with taco seasoning or a smoky chipotle rub before smashing. After flipping, top with Pepper Jack cheese and a spoonful of fire-roasted green chillies. Layer with guacamole, pickled red onions and a squirt of lime crema.

THE SMOKEHOUSE STACK

Where burger meets BBQ, slow and smoky wins the day

This is a full barbecue platter stacked between 2 buns. Top your seared patty with smoked Cheddar, pulled pork and a drizzle of your favourite BBQ sauce. Add crispy fried onions or coleslaw for texture and tang.

THE MASALA SMASH

Fragrant, spicy and packed with flavour

Mix a small spoon of garam masala, ginger-garlic paste and chilli powder into the beef before forming. Top with paneer or spicy cheese, and let it melt.

Serve on a butter-toasted pav bun or brioche with mint chutney, red onion rings, tomato slices and a swipe of tamarind sauce for a tangy punch.

THE CHIMICHURRI SMASH

Meaty, tangy and loaded with Latin flair

Fresh, bold and made for steak lovers. Season the beef with salt, pepper and smoked paprika before smashing. Top with provolone cheese and spoon on some chimichurri as it melts. Serve with grilled red peppers, rocket and thinly sliced red onion. A toasted crusty roll (or classic brioche) brushed with garlic butter seals the deal.

THE AUSSIE BURGER WITH THE LOT

Straight from the land Down Under

Messy, massive and completely glorious, this is a true Aussie BBQ icon.

Regular smash patty, seasoned with salt and pepper. After the cheese, add grilled pineapple, beetroot slices, a fried egg, bacon and onion. Finish with tomato sauce (ketchup), lettuce and tomato on a toasted bun.

THE DUBLINER SMASH (Irish-inspired)

Hearty, rich and perfect for cold evenings

Finish this barbecue with a creamy pint of Guinness and a good story. It's Irish comfort food, but burger-fied.

Stick with the classic beef smash patty, seasoned with sea salt and freshly ground black pepper. Top with a thick slice of extra mature Cheddar cheese – it's sharp, nutty and melts beautifully. Add a layer of crispy rashers (Irish-style back bacon) for a salty, meaty punch, and spoon on some caramelised Guinness onions slow-cooked in stout until sticky and sweet.

SWE
EET Sw
ET SW
Sweet S
SWE

BBQ CHOCOLATE MUFFINS *in* ORANGE SKINS

Fudgy chocolate muffins steamed inside orange skins on the BBQ – citrusy, smoky and ridiculously fun for all ages

 Prep Time: 20 minutes

 Cook Time: 20–25 minutes

SERVES 6

6 large oranges
100g (3½oz) unsalted butter
150g (5oz) dark chocolate, roughly chopped
2 large eggs
100g (3½oz) caster sugar
1 tsp vanilla extract
75g (3oz) self-raising flour
25g (1oz) cocoa powder
Pinch of salt
Chocolate chips or chunks, mini marshmallows or a spoonful of Nutella (optional)

Think campfire vibes with a gourmet twist – this one's ideal for kids and grown-ups alike, whether you're at a festival or just firing up the backyard grill. Perfect with a scoop of vanilla ice cream or a drizzle of orange liqueur for grown-up flair.

Prep

Carefully slice the top 1–2cm (½–¾in) off each orange (like a lid). Use a small knife and spoon to hollow out the inside, removing as much pulp as possible without piercing the skin. Save the juice for another use, such as a cocktail. Wrap the base of each orange in a little foil to stabilise them on the barbecue.

Melt the butter and chocolate together in a saucepan over a low heat or in a bowl set over a pan of simmering water, not letting the base of the bowl touch the water. Let it cool slightly.

In a mixing bowl, whisk the eggs and sugar until pale and fluffy. Stir in the vanilla extract, then add the cooled chocolate mixture. Sift in the flour, cocoa powder and salt. Fold gently to combine. If you like, stir through chocolate chips or add a surprise filling like a spoon of Nutella to each muffin centre.

Set the barbecue to indirect heat at around 180–200°C (350–400°F).

Grill

Spoon the batter into each hollowed-out orange, filling them about three-quarters full. Set them upright on the barbecue, close the lid and cook for 20–25 minutes until the muffin tops are set and spring back to the touch.

Serve

Carefully remove the oranges from the barbecue. Let them cool for a few minutes, then unwrap the base foil and dig in with a spoon straight from the peel, or slice them open for a gooey centre reveal.

SMOKY GRILLED PEACHES with COINTREAU & ROSEMARY

BBQ dessert at its finest

 Prep Time: 10 minutes

 Cook Time: 10 minutes

SERVES 4

- 4 ripe peaches, halved and stoned
- Olive oil, for brushing
- 8 tbsp runny honey
- 175ml (6fl oz) Cointreau
- 1 tbsp finely chopped fresh rosemary
- Crème fraîche or thick Greek-style yoghurt, to serve

This one's all about letting simple ingredients shine over the flames. Inspired by a peachy dessert I tried in southern Spain, I've swapped the sherry for Cointreau, a bold orange liqueur that lifts the sweetness of the peaches and pairs beautifully with honey and rosemary. Grill the fruit until blistered and caramelised, let the Cointreau bubble into a syrup, and serve warm with a spoonful of crème fraîche or thick yoghurt. It's sunshine on a plate and perfect for a barbecue party finish.

Prep
Fire up your barbecue to medium-high heat (200–220°C/400–425°F) and oil the grates to stop the fruit from sticking.

Grill
Brush the peach halves with a bit of oil and place them cut-side down. Let them char for 3–4 minutes until you've got those dark caramelised grill marks. Flip the peaches over, spoon a bit of honey into each centre, then pour a splash of Cointreau into each one. Sprinkle with chopped rosemary and close the lid. Cook for another 4–5 minutes until the peaches soften and the Cointreau gently bubbles into a citrusy glaze.

Serve
Lift the peaches carefully off the grill, drizzle over any sticky syrup left behind, and serve warm with a spoonful of crème fraîche or thick yoghurt.

→ **Add Crunch:** Finish with a sprinkle of toasted hazelnuts or crushed amaretti biscuits for extra texture.

→ **Switch the Fruit:** This also works brilliantly with nectarines or apricots - just adjust the cook time slightly (softer fruits tend to grill a bit faster).

BOOZY GRILLED RUM-INFUSED PINEAPPLE

Cocktail in hand, this is summer BBQ dessert done right

 Prep Time: 20 minutes, plus 1 hour marinating

 Cook Time: 10 minutes

SERVES 4–6

| 3 tbsp desiccated coconut |
| 1 tbsp dark brown sugar |
| ¼ tsp sea salt |
| ½ tsp freshly ground black pepper |
| 1 ripe pineapple, peeled, cored and sliced into 8 long spears |
| Oil, for brushing |
| Vanilla or coconut ice cream, to serve |

FOR THE RUM BUTTER

| 100g (3½oz) unsalted butter, softened |
| 2 tbsp dark or spiced rum |
| 1 tbsp dark brown sugar |

Imagine you're in the Caribbean on a warm, breezy evening, surrounded by the intoxicating scents of rum and tropical fruits. This recipe brings that carefree island vibe to your garden.

This dessert takes inspiration from the vibrant flavours of Jamaica – where rum reigns supreme and fresh tropical fruits are a daily indulgence. Grilled pineapple has long been a tropical favourite, but when infused with the dark Jamaican rum butter it transforms into a truly decadent treat.

Prep

First make the butter. In a bowl, mash together the softened butter, rum and brown sugar until smooth. Chill until ready to use, or freeze for a firmer slice-on-top finish.

In a dry pan over a medium heat, toast the coconut until golden and fragrant, stirring often – don't walk away. Set aside to cool.

Mix the remaining brown sugar, salt and pepper in a small bowl and sprinkle over the pineapple spears in a dish or tray. Let them sit at room temperature for 1 hour, turning halfway and brushing the juices over them.

Set your barbecue for direct heat, aiming for around 200–230°C (400–450°F). Clean and oil the grates to stop any sticking.

Grill

Place the spears straight onto the hot grates. Grill for 8–10 minutes, turning every few minutes until you've got char marks and a caramelised glaze. Keep the lid down for best results – you want that smoky edge.

As soon as the spears come off the grill, spoon over the rum butter so it melts into all the nooks and charred edges. Sprinkle with the toasted coconut.

Serve

Pile onto a platter with scoops of vanilla ice cream and let the warm pineapple start to melt the cold ice cream.

➔ **Fruit Twist:** Swap the pineapple for ripe mango cheeks or banana halves.
➔ **Warm It Up:** Add a pinch of ground allspice or cinnamon to the rum butter for more warmth.
➔ **Make It Boozier:** Drizzle an extra teaspoon of rum over each spear before serving.

KEY LIME PIE
(BBQ-Friendly No-Bake Version)

 Prep Time: 25 minutes

 Chill Time: 4–6 hours or overnight

 Cook Time: 8–10 minutes (optional)

SERVES 8

FOR THE BASE
250g (9oz) digestive biscuits, crushed

100g (3½oz) unsalted butter, melted

Zest of 1 lime, plus extra for garnish

Pinch of salt

FOR THE FILLING
397g (14oz) tin of sweetened condensed milk

400g (14oz) full-fat cream cheese

Zest and juice of 10 limes (around 175ml/6fl oz juice)

TO SERVE (optional)
Whipped cream

Sharp, creamy and cooling, this no-bake key lime pie sets in the fridge on a buttery biscuit base, leaving the BBQ free for the main event. Zesty, creamy and just the right amount of indulgent, this one's inspired by beach stops down the Florida Keys and lazy barbecue evenings where dessert needs to be effortless.

Prep
Blitz the biscuits into fine crumbs in a food processor or blender, then stir in the melted butter, lime zest and a pinch of salt.

Press the mixture into a tart tin (about 20–23cm/8–9in) lined with baking parchment or use a springform tin for easy removal. Press it down firmly with the back of a spoon. For a bit of extra crunch, pop the base into a barbecue (indirect heat) or oven at 180°C/160°C fan (350°F) for 8–10 minutes, then cool.

In a large bowl, whisk together the condensed milk, cream cheese and lime zest and juice until smooth. Pour the filling over the biscuit base, smoothing the top. Cover and chill in the fridge for at least 4–6 hours, preferably overnight, until set.

Serve
Just before serving, garnish with extra lime zest, lime curls or whipped cream. Serve cold and keep it in the fridge until it's time to slice, it disappears quickly once it hits the table.

SKILLET COOKIE DOUGH

The ultimate BBQ dessert – crispy on the edges, molten in the middle

Prep Time: 10 minutes

Cook Time: 20–25 minutes

Equipment: 25–30cm (10–12in) cast-iron skillet

SERVES 6–8

- 170g (6oz) unsalted butter, softened
- 150g (5oz) soft light brown sugar
- 50g (2oz) granulated sugar
- 1 large egg, plus 1 yolk
- 1½ tsp vanilla extract
- 225g (8oz) plain flour
- ½ tsp bicarbonate of soda
- ½ tsp salt
- 200g (7oz) chocolate chips or chopped chocolate (dark, milk or a mix)
- Sea salt flakes, toasted nuts or chunks of honeycomb (optional)

This is what happens when your barbecue ends on a high. Inspired by those giant, American-style cookies served warm in cast-iron skillets, this recipe is built for feasting. You can load it with chocolate chips, chunks or whatever you fancy. Toss it on the barbecue over indirect heat with the lid down or bake it indoors if you must, but either way, don't forget the ice cream.

Prep

Cream the butter and both sugars in a bowl until fluffy and pale. Add the egg, egg yolk and vanilla and mix until smooth.

In a separate bowl, whisk together the flour, bicarbonate of soda and salt. Gradually fold the dry mix into the wet until a dough forms. Stir through most of the chocolate chips, saving a handful to press on top later.

Preheat your barbecue for indirect cooking at around 180–190°C (350–375°F). If baking indoors, set the oven to 180°C/160°C fan (350°F).

Press the dough into a greased or parchment-lined cast-iron skillet, spreading it evenly. Press the reserved chocolate chips into the top. Add any extras like sea salt or nuts now if you're using them.

Grill

Pop the skillet into the barbecue with the lid closed, or into the oven, if using. Bake for 20–25 minutes, until the edges are golden and set but the centre is still soft. Don't overbake – it'll keep cooking in the pan once removed from the heat.

Serve

Let it sit for 5–10 minutes before diving in. Serve straight from the skillet with scoops of vanilla ice cream and spoons all round.

➔ **S'mores Style:** Swap 50g (2oz) of flour for crushed digestive biscuits or graham crackers, and scatter marshmallows on top halfway through baking.

➔ **Peanut Butter Swirl:** Dollop and swirl a few teaspoons of peanut butter through the dough before baking.

➔ **Bourbon Chocolate:** Stir a tablespoon of bourbon into the dough for an adult twist.

PEACH & MASCARPONE FRENCH TOAST

A sweet start from the grill

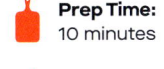 **Prep Time:** 10 minutes

 **Cook Time:** 10–15 minutes

SERVES 2–4

Ingredients
1 tub (approx. 250g/9oz) mascarpone
1 tsp vanilla extract
4 thick-cut brioche slices (or bread of your choice)
4 eggs, whisked with a splash of milk
400g (14oz) tin of sliced peaches in syrup, or use 400g (14oz) fresh peaches (see Fresh Swap)
Handful of mixed berries, such as blueberries or raspberries
Caramel sauce, for drizzling

This indulgent barbecue breakfast (or dessert) transforms classic French toast into a decadent dish layered with grilled peaches, whipped vanilla mascarpone and a drizzle of caramel sauce. It's comfort food at its best – rich, golden and just the right amount of over-the-top. Using tinned peaches adds a syrupy caramelisation that brings everything together, making it the ultimate sweet treat straight off the grill.

Prep

Set your barbecue to medium–high heat (180–230°C/350–450°F) and place a cast-iron griddle or plancha over the flames. Allow it to get nice and hot.

In a small bowl, whip the mascarpone with the vanilla extract until smooth and airy. Set aside in a cool place or chill slightly for extra firmness.

Dip each slice of brioche into the egg and milk mixture, making sure both sides are fully coated.

Grill

Add the brioche slices to the hot griddle and cook for 2–3 minutes per side, or until golden and slightly crisp. Once done, move to a cooler side of the grill or keep warm.

Pour the tinned peaches and all their syrup directly onto the griddle. Allow them to bubble and caramelise without moving them too much – this helps create colour and syrupy edges that add loads of flavour. Flip gently once to sear both sides.

Serve

Plate the grilled French toast slices and top each with a generous spoonful of the vanilla mascarpone. Pile on the warm caramelised peaches, scatter with fresh berries, and finish with a generous drizzle of caramel sauce.

Serve immediately with a strong coffee, a fork, and zero guilt.

→ **Boozy Brunch Vibes:** Add a splash of bourbon or dark rum to the peach syrup before grilling for an adult twist.

→ **Spiced Up:** Sprinkle a little ground cinnamon or cardamom over the peaches while they caramelise for extra depth.

→ **Nutty Crunch:** Crushed pecans or toasted almonds add texture and a nutty richness to balance the sweetness.

→ **Fresh Swap:** If using fresh peaches, slice them thinly and toss with a little brown sugar and lemon juice before grilling to help mimic the syrupy glaze.

PEACH COBBLER IN TIN COFFEE CUPS

Juicy peaches bubbling under a buttery cobbler lid

Prep Time: 20 minutes

Cook Time: 30–35 minutes

SERVES 6–8

FOR THE FRUIT FILLING

- 8 ripe peaches, stoned and sliced into wedges
- 1 vanilla pod, halved and seeds scraped
- Zest of 1 lime
- Zest and juice of 1 orange
- 40g (1½oz) soft brown sugar
- 1 tsp ground cinnamon
- 1 tsp ground ginger
- 2 tbsp bourbon, plus a splash for finishing, or 2 tbsp maple syrup or honey

FOR THE COBBLER TOPPING

- 40g (1½oz) pine nuts
- 100g (3½oz) self-raising flour
- 50g (2oz) caster sugar
- Pinch of sea salt
- 100g (3½oz) unsalted butter, chilled and cubed

TO SERVE

- Icing sugar, for dusting
- Good-quality vanilla ice cream

I first came across this style of cobbler while road-tripping with my family through southern Florida, when after a meal our kids were served sweet, juicy peaches baked in tin coffee cups with a buttery topping and a scoop of melting ice cream. It was rustic, charming and downright addictive… and definitely too good just for the kids to enjoy by themselves, so we had to get in on the action too!

This version gets the barbecue treatment. Served in old-school tin mugs, they're easy to make ahead, look great on a serving board and taste even better cooked over fire. The peaches are soaked in citrus and warm spice, topped with a nutty crumb and finished with a scoop of vanilla ice cream that melts into every bite.

Prep

Preheat your barbecue to 190°C (375°F) and set it up for indirect cooking. Line up 6–8 tin coffee cups on a tray.

In a large bowl, toss the sliced peaches with the vanilla seeds, lime zest, orange zest and juice, brown sugar, cinnamon and ginger. Add the bourbon or maple syrup at this stage. Mix gently until coated. Spoon the peach mixture into the tin cups, distributing evenly.

Blitz the pine nuts in a food processor until finely ground. Add the flour, sugar and salt, then pulse in the cold butter until the mix resembles fine crumbs.

Grill

Place the cups (on the tray) onto the barbecue. Close the lid and bake for 15 minutes until the peaches soften.

Take the cups off the heat. Stir in a small splash of water (about 1 tablespoon per cup) to loosen the juices. Spoon a generous mound of cobbler mix onto each cup of fruit.

Return the tray of cobblers to the barbecue and bake for another 15–20 minutes until the tops are golden, crisp at the edges and bubbling underneath.

Serve

Let them cool slightly, then dust with icing sugar and serve warm with a scoop of vanilla ice cream. Dig in when the cobbler is still warm and the ice cream starts to melt.

➔ **Seasonal Swap:** Use tart apples instead of peaches and swap in nutmeg for the ginger.

RUBS

SIGNATURE SPG STEAK RUB

Salt, pepper and garlic balanced for big crust and clean beef flavour

MAKES ENOUGH FOR 6–8 STEAKS

GREAT FOR:

Ribeye, sirloin, T-bone or even steak burgers

2 tbsp coarse sea salt or flaky Maldon salt

2 tbsp freshly ground black pepper (medium grind)

1 tbsp garlic granules (not garlic powder)

1 tbsp onion granules, or toasted onion powder for depth

1 tsp smoked paprika (optional, but adds a hint of colour and smoke)

½ tsp mustard powder

½ tsp dried rosemary or thyme (optional, adds a herby twist)

This rub draws inspiration from classic Texas-style simplicity but gets a small lift from toasted onion powder, mustard powder and a pinch of smoked paprika, bringing a balanced edge without overshadowing the meat. Ideal for anyone who wants to let the beef do the talking.

Combine all the ingredients and add to a small jar with a lid. Store in a cool, dark place. This blend will keep for up to 3 months, but chances are you'll use it long before then.

How to Use It:

Pat the steak dry with kitchen paper, then sprinkle the rub generously on both sides, roughly 1 teaspoon per side for a thick-cut steak. Let it sit at room temperature for 30–40 minutes before grilling or reverse-searing. This gives the salt time to penetrate the meat while the rest of the rub builds a crust when seared over high heat.

BRISKET RUB: THE FLAVOUR FOUNDATION

Pepper-forward rub that builds bark without masking the meat

A good brisket rub sets the stage for that deep, crave-worthy bark and layers of flavour. This blend strikes a balance between smoky, sweet and savoury with just a touch of heat. You can tweak it to match your mood – or the crowd you're cooking for.

What's Inside:

Smokiness
Paprika is the backbone here. For classic flavour use sweet paprika, but if you want to dial up that campfire vibe, go with smoked paprika for an extra layer of depth.

Sweetness
I love using granulated maple sugar – it brings just the right sweetness with a hint of natural richness. Don't have any on hand? Coconut sugar is a great swap, with subtle caramel notes, or use brown sugar if you're not worried about refined sugars. It's all good.

Warm Savoury Backbone
This is where the rub really comes alive:
- Garlic powder
- Onion powder
- Ground cumin
- Cayenne pepper (enough to warm things up)
- Kosher salt
- Freshly ground black pepper

Make It Your Own:
If you're after more heat, bump up the cayenne to taste. Want it earthier? Add a little mustard powder or ground coriander. You're in control!

MY SIGNATURE BRISKET RUB

Pepper-heavy backbone with subtle warmth and a dry dark bark

Prep Time: 5 minutes, plus overnight marinating

MAKES ENOUGH FOR 1 WHOLE PACKER OF BRISKET

2 tbsp smoked paprika, or sweet paprika for a milder flavour
2 tbsp granulated brown sugar
2 tbsp garlic powder
1 tbsp onion powder
2 tbsp kosher salt
1½ tbsp freshly ground black pepper
1 tsp ground cumin
½ tsp cayenne pepper

Smoky, sweet and savoury with just enough kick, this rub builds a bold bark and deep flavour on any brisket.

Prep
In a small bowl, mix all the ingredients until evenly combined.

Pat your brisket dry with kitchen paper, then coat generously with the rub, pressing/pushing it into every nook and edge. Don't rub it with your hand as it will give an uneven distribution of the rub.

Let it sit for at least 30 minutes at room temperature or wrap and refrigerate overnight for a deeper flavour.

Grill
Smoke, barbecue, slow-cook or roast as desired.

Optional Add-ins for Heat Lovers:
→ Add an extra ½–1 teaspoon cayenne pepper for a spicier kick.
→ Stir in ½ teaspoon chipotle powder for smoky heat.
→ Sprinkle in ¼ teaspoon crushed dried chilli flakes for texture and slow-building fire.

Want a Coffee Twist?
Add 1 teaspoon finely ground espresso for a bold, earthy flavour that works beautifully with brisket bark.

ALL-PURPOSE CHIPOTLE BEEF RUB

Texas smoke meets Mexican soul

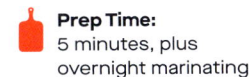
Prep Time:
5 minutes, plus overnight marinating

MAKES ENOUGH FOR 1 WHOLE PACKER OF BRISKET

GREAT FOR:
Brisket, ribs, chuck roasts, steaks

PAIRS WITH:
Bourbon BBQ sauce, smoky salsas, citrus slaws

- 2 tbsp sea salt (fine or flaky depending on your texture preference)
- 2 tbsp dark brown sugar
- 1 tbsp smoked paprika
- 1 tsp chipotle powder
- 1 tsp ground cumin
- 1 tsp ancho chilli powder
- ½ tsp garlic powder
- ½ tsp onion powder
- ¼ tsp cayenne pepper

This rub is all about bold flavours – sweet, smoky and just the right touch of heat. It's inspired by those long, slow-cooked briskets you get deep in Texas, but with a whisper of Mexican influence, thanks to the chipotle and ancho chilli. I first played around with this combo after a road trip that took in some Texas BBQ joints and plenty of Tex-Mex smoky street food trucks in Austin, and it just stuck. The result? A bark that's rich, spiced and totally unforgettable.

Use it on anything from full-packer briskets to beef ribs, short rib burgers, chuck roasts or even grilled portobellos. Just don't be shy with it.

Combine all the ingredients and add to a small jar with a lid. Store in a cool, dark place. This blend will keep for up to 3 months, but chances are you'll use it long before then.

How to Use It:

Apply with purpose – Pat your meat dry and give it a light coat of oil or mustard, if needed, just enough for the rub to stick. Shake your rub from a height for even coverage and don't forget the edges. Use a tray to catch the excess, especially useful if you're seasoning multiple cuts.

Layer if needed – For bigger cuts like brisket, start with a base of SPG (salt, pepper, garlic) and layer this on top to build depth. You could go 70 per cent SPG, 30 per cent of this chipotle rub for balance.

→ **Sweet Heat**: Add 1 teaspoon ground cinnamon and swap cayenne for hot paprika.
→ **Espresso Kick**: Stir in 1 teaspoon finely ground coffee for smoky beefy depth.
→ **Herb Crust**: Add 1 teaspoon dried oregano or thyme.

MAPLE & MUSTARD PORK RUB
Southern sweet meets mustard heat

GREAT FOR:
Pork ribs, Boston butts, pork belly, chops or loin

PAIRS WITH:
Maple-mustard glaze, apple cider BBQ sauce, pickled slaw

This one's got Southern soul running right through it. Think sticky pork ribs cooked low 'n' slow over maple wood, finished with that signature mustard tang you'll find from Carolina to Kentucky. The mustard powder cuts through the sweetness of brown sugar, while smoked paprika and allspice bring a mellow warmth.

It's a rub that's just as at home on a Sunday roast pork shoulder as it is dusted onto chops midweek or ribs heading onto the grill. Sweet, tangy and bold, it brings a bit of flair without overcomplicating things.

- 2 tbsp sea salt
- 2 tbsp light brown sugar
- 1 tbsp mustard powder
- 1 tbsp smoked paprika
- 1 tsp garlic powder
- ½ tsp ground allspice
- ½ tsp coarse black pepper

Combine all the ingredients and add to a small jar with a lid. Store in a cool, dark place. This blend will keep for up to 3 months, but chances are you'll use it long before then.

How to Use It:

Prep your meat – Pat the pork dry and lightly oil if needed, this helps the rub stick evenly. Lay your meat in a tray to catch excess rub (and save your surfaces).

Season from a height – Sprinkle the rub over your meat from around 30cm (12in) above, this helps it distribute evenly like a fine dusting. Don't forget the edges and all the underside.

→ **Extra Maple Hit:** Add 1 teaspoon maple sugar or powdered maple syrup if you have it.

→ **For Bark Lovers:** Add ½ teaspoon cracked coriander seed or fennel for texture and bite.

→ **Chilli Twist:** Toss in ½ teaspoon cayenne or chipotle for a little back-end heat.

CITRUS HERB SEAFOOD RUB

Bright, zesty, beach-ready barbecue flavour

GREAT FOR:
Fish fillets, prawn skewers, grilled calamari, lobster tails

PAIRS WITH:
Lemon butter, dill aioli, charred corn salad

This rub brings a taste of the coast straight to your grill. It's crisp, fragrant and made for seafood, whether you're grilling a whole fish over fire or flash-searing scallops on a plancha.

The citrus and herbs lift delicate seafood without overpowering it, while just a hint of smoked paprika adds depth if you're cooking over flame. Perfect for keeping things fresh, light and barbecue board-worthy.

- 2 tbsp sea salt
- 1 tbsp dried dill or parsley, or a mix of both
- 1 tbsp garlic powder
- 1 tsp finely grated lemon zest (dried or fresh)
- ½ tsp white pepper
- ¼ tsp smoked paprika (optional, adds subtle depth)

Combine all the ingredients and add to a small jar with a lid. Store in a cool, dark place. This blend will keep for up to 3 months, but chances are you'll use it long before then.

How to Use It:

Dry your seafood – Use kitchen paper to pat the fish or shellfish dry as this helps the rub stick and gives you a better sear.

Apply lightly and evenly – Sprinkle from a height for even coverage. Seafood doesn't need a heavy coat, just enough to season and accent the natural flavour.

Let it sit briefly – Allow the rub to sit for 10–15 minutes before grilling as this gives the citrus oils time to infuse without curing the protein too much.

→ `Orange or lime zest:` These can be used instead or as well as the lemon, for a different citrus note.

→ `Crushed fennel seed:` Add ½ teaspoon for a subtle aniseed lift.

SAUCES & CONDIMENTS

GUACAMOLE
The OG green gold

 **Prep Time:** 10 minutes

SERVES 4

- 2 ripe avocados, peeled, halved and stoned
- 1 tbsp fresh lime juice
- ½ tsp flaky sea salt
- 1 small red chilli, finely diced (seeds in or out, your call)
- 1 garlic clove, finely minced
- 2 ripe tomatoes, deseeded and diced
- 1 small red onion, finely chopped
- 1 tbsp roughly chopped fresh coriander
- Pinch of ground cumin (optional)

This one's got a special place in our story. It all started on our honeymoon in Mexico, when we were sitting on an upturned crate under a scrap of tarp, cold beer in hand and a plastic bowl of the freshest guacamole you could imagine. No sourdough, no avocado toast trend, just ripe avocados mashed with lime, chilli and tomato, eaten with salty tortilla chips straight off the grill. That first bite was like a revelation, and we've been chasing that flavour ever since. This is our go-to version, a nod to that memory. It's simple, bold and built for barbecues, spoon it over fire-kissed prawns, burgers or just keep it classic with chips and cold drinks.

Prep
Pop the avocados into a bowl and mash with a fork to your preferred consistency – chunky or smooth, it's up to you.

Stir in the lime juice and salt first, to wake the avocado up. Then fold in the chilli, garlic, tomatoes, onion and coriander. If using cumin, add it now.

Want more heat? Add a little more chilli. Needs brightness? Another squeeze of lime never hurts.

Serve
Spoon it into a bowl and serve immediately with charred tortilla chips, grilled meats or straight onto tacos. Best eaten fresh, but it'll keep in the fridge for a few hours with the stone nestled back in to help prevent browning.

- → **Sweet Heat:** Add grilled corn, chopped mango or pineapple for a tropical twist.
- → **Creamy Kick:** Stir in a spoonful of soured cream or scatter with crumbled feta.
- → **Smoky Vibes:** Add a pinch of smoked paprika or char your tomatoes and onion on the grill first for a richer flavour.

IRISH CIDER APPLE & HONEY BBQ SAUCE
A sweet and tangy summer classic

Prep Time: 5 minutes
Cook Time: 25–30 minutes

MAKES ABOUT 300ML (10FL OZ)

250ml (9fl oz) Magners Irish cider	
45g (2oz) tomato paste	
60ml (2½fl oz) apple cider vinegar	
1 tbsp honey	
2 tbsp low-sodium soy sauce	
½ tsp chilli powder	
¼ tsp ground cinnamon	
¼ tsp black pepper	
Pinch of cayenne pepper	

There's nothing like those warm, sunny summer days when the barbecue is slow-cooking away, filling the air with irresistible smells, and the only thing missing is a chilled glass of Magners Irish Cider over ice.

A nod to the iconic Irish cider, this sauce brings that same crisp, refreshing vibe to your meats with a perfect balance of sweet, tangy and just the right amount of heat. It's not just a sauce – it's a memory in a jar. The cider gives it a unique depth, while the honey and apple cider vinegar add a beautiful sweetness and tang. Add a pinch of cayenne and cinnamon for warmth and you've got a sauce that transforms anything from sausages to ribs into something special. While the recipe is simple, it's got endless potential. Try it as a glaze for grilled chicken, drizzled over roasted veggies or served alongside burgers. You can also take it up a notch with a dash of smoked paprika or a squeeze of fresh lime for extra zest.

Prep
Put all the ingredients except the cayenne into a small stainless-steel saucepan.

Cook
Bring to a gentle bubble and cook, uncovered, over a medium-low heat until the sauce has thickened and reduced by half. Add the cayenne little by little until you get your desired heat level.

Serve
Pour into a jar and set aside. Transfer the hot sauce into sterilised jars/bottles, cool for 2 hours, then keep refrigerated for 2–3 weeks.

➔ **Add Smoky Depth:** For a deeper, richer flavour, add a splash of bourbon or Irish whiskey. The caramelised notes from the spirit will add another layer of complexity to the sauce, giving it a smoky, almost charred edge that's perfect for grilled meats.

➔ **Citrus Zing:** Try adding a squeeze of fresh orange or lemon juice, or even some zest. The citrus will give the sauce an extra burst of freshness that complements the apple cider vinegar and balances out the sweetness from the honey.

➔ **Spicy Kick:** If you like more heat, fresh chopped red or green chillies (such as serrano or jalapeño) can add an exciting kick to the sauce. You could also experiment with chipotle peppers in adobo for a smoky, spicy depth.

➔ **Herby Freshness:** Stir in some finely chopped fresh herbs like basil or thyme for a fresh, herbal note.

SWEET & SMOKY BOURBON BBQ SAUCE
Sticky, boozy and built for the flames!

Prep Time: 5 minutes

Cook Time: 40–45 minutes

MAKES ABOUT 480ML (16FL OZ)

- 240ml (8fl oz) ketchup
- 120ml (4fl oz) reduced-sodium soy sauce
- 140ml (5fl oz) honey
- 60ml (2½fl oz) bourbon (I love Buffalo Trace, Jack Daniel's, or whatever's handy)
- 2 garlic cloves, crushed
- 1½ tsp of your favourite BBQ spice rub (smoky paprika, garlic, onion, brown sugar blend works well, or see pages 224–9)
- ½ tsp freshly ground black pepper

This one's a no-fuss classic that's earned its spot in our barbecue rotation. It's dead simple to make, keeps beautifully and goes with just about anything you throw on the grill. A true keeper, this sauce is begging to be brushed onto everything, whether you're glazing a stack of baby backs or slathering it on a burger, it brings serious Southern States swagger to the party. And because it's a little bit sweet, a little bit sticky and a whole lot boozy, you'll be tempted to keep a jar of it on standby all summer long.

Prep
In a medium stainless-steel saucepan over a low heat, combine the ketchup, soy sauce, honey, garlic, BBQ rub and black pepper. Stir to bring everything together.

Cook
Let the sauce bubble gently for 40–45 minutes, stirring every so often to stop it catching. It should reduce slightly and take on a rich, glossy texture.

Serve
Stir in the bourbon, then remove from the heat and let it cool slightly before pouring into a sterilised jam jar or bottle. Pop it in the fridge, where it'll thicken even more and deepen in flavour. It will keep in the fridge for 2–3 weeks.

How to Use It:
Glaze ribs or wings in the final few minutes of grilling.
Drizzle over pulled pork sandwiches or brisket buns.
Use as a cheeky burger base sauce or even as a dip for BBQ wedges.

→ **Add Tang:** Add a splash of apple cider vinegar if you like it with more tang.
→ **Smoky Hit:** A teaspoon of smoked paprika or chipotle paste will dial up the smoky vibes.
→ **Make It Zingy:** Stir in a tablespoon of Dijon mustard for a sharp, zippy finish.

MINT & PARSLEY SAUCE for SMOKED LAMB RACKS

Fresh, fiery and full of herb power

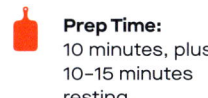 **Prep Time:** 10 minutes, plus 10–15 minutes resting

MAKES ABOUT 240ML (8FL OZ)

- 2 garlic cloves, roughly chopped
- 30g (1oz) fresh mint leaves
- 30g (1oz) fresh flat-leaf parsley
- 2 tbsp red wine vinegar
- ½ tsp sea salt or kosher salt
- ¼ tsp dried chilli flakes (adjust to heat preference)
- 6 tbsp extra virgin olive oil

Lamb and mint is one of those iconic flavour pairings, but this isn't your Sunday roast-style mint jelly. This mint chimichurri takes its cues from Argentine asado culture, where sauces are sharp, fresh and meant to be spooned generously over grilled meats straight off the coals.

Use it with lamb racks simply seasoned with SPG (salt, pepper, garlic) and cooked over wood or charcoal. Drizzle it over the top, serve it on the side, or mop it up with flatbread. It's fast to make, even faster to disappear.

Prep

Add the garlic, mint, parsley, red wine vinegar, salt and chilli flakes to a food processor or blender. Pulse a few times to combine.

Slowly drizzle in the olive oil while blending until you get a loose, spoonable sauce. Scrape down the sides as needed to get everything nicely chopped and emulsified. Give it a taste, add more salt and a splash more vinegar or extra chilli if you want it bolder. It should be fresh, tangy and just a little bit fiery.

Serve

Pour into a bowl and let it sit at room temperature for 10–15 minutes to allow the flavours to come together. Spoon generously over grilled lamb or use it as a dipping sauce.

→ **Zing It Up:** Add the zest of half a lemon or a squeeze of juice for extra brightness.
→ **Texture Swap:** Mix in a few finely chopped capers for salty depth or a spoon of finely diced shallot for more punch.
→ **Herb Blend:** Add in a handful of fresh coriander or tarragon for a different spin.

PINEAPPLE & CHILLI SALSA

A sweet-heat hit with a tropical twist

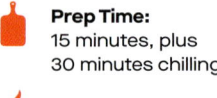

Prep Time:
15 minutes, plus 30 minutes chilling

Cook Time:
8 minutes

SERVES 4–6

1 large pineapple, peeled, cored and cut into 1cm (½in) thick slices
1 red pepper, finely diced
75g (3oz) red onion, finely diced
1 jalapeño, finely chopped
Juice of 1 lime
1 tbsp chopped fresh coriander
1 tsp honey
1 tsp black pepper
1 tsp kosher salt
½ tsp ground cumin
1 tbsp extra virgin olive oil
Tortilla chips, to serve

Your barbecue just got a tropical upgrade! This salsa is summer in a bowl. Inspired by the vibrant flavours of the tropics – think Hawaiian barbecue meets Mexican street food – this salsa is all about contrast: sweet, smoky, spicy and zesty all at once.

It first hit our radar during a trip to Maui, where we enjoyed lunch at a beachside old-school barbecue pit, where the grilled pineapple and chilli-laced sauce added a wonderful pop to the dishes we enjoyed, and we were captivated. Since then, we've made it a go-to for pork, chicken, fish tacos or just a big bowl of tortilla chips.

The key is grilling that pineapple until it's caramelised and golden, adding an irresistible depth of flavour. From there, everything gets tossed together for a fresh, fiery salsa that's as perfect on a hot summer's day as it is beside your barbecue favourites.

Grill
Grill the pineapple slices over a medium-high heat until charred and caramelised, about 3–4 minutes per side. Let cool slightly, then dice.

Prep
In a bowl, combine the grilled pineapple with the red pepper, onion and jalapeño.

Add the lime juice, coriander, honey, pepper, salt, cumin and olive oil. Toss well to combine. Chill for at least 30 minutes to let the flavours mingle.

Serve
Serve with tortilla chips or spoon over grilled meats, tacos or burgers.

CHUNKY TOMATO RELISH

A bold backyard classic

Prep Time: 10 minutes
Cook Time: 25 minutes

MAKES ABOUT 480ML (16FL OZ)

- 2 tbsp olive oil
- 1 onion, grated
- 2 tsp freshly crushed garlic
- 400g (14oz) tin of chopped tomatoes
- 1 tbsp Worcestershire sauce
- 1 tbsp tomato paste
- 75g (3oz) golden syrup
- 8 medium dill pickles, diced
- 1 red pepper, roasted, peeled, deseeded and diced
- ½ tsp freshly ground black pepper
- ¼ tsp ground allspice
- ¼ tsp sweet paprika
- 2 fresh bay leaves
- 1 tsp Dijon mustard
- 1 tsp sea salt
- 240ml (8fl oz) water

Every backyard hero needs a signature condiment, and this chunky tomato relish might just be yours. It's packed with big, bold flavours and just the right amount of tang.

This isn't your smooth, ketchup-style sauce. It's chunky, savoury, slightly sweet and bursting with textures from dill pickles and roasted peppers. It's the perfect topping for burgers, sausages, grilled chicken or even stirred into scrambled eggs the next morning (if there's any left!). Slather it, scoop it, share it, this relish is a total game changer.

The best part? It keeps well in the fridge, so you'll always have a spoonful of magic ready to fire up your favourites.

Cook

Heat the olive oil in a stainless-steel saucepan over a medium heat. Sauté the grated onion for 2–3 minutes just until translucent. Add the garlic and cook for another minute. Stir in the chopped tomatoes, Worcestershire sauce and tomato paste and simmer for 5 minutes. Add all the remaining ingredients and stir well. Simmer gently for 15 minutes, stirring occasionally.

Serve

Remove from the heat and let cool slightly. Remove and discard the bay leaves. Spoon into an airtight container and store in the fridge for up to 6 weeks.

FIERY FRESH SALSA
A taste of Mexico at home

Prep Time:
10 minutes, plus
15 minutes resting

SERVES 4–6

- ½ white onion, roughly chopped
- 2–3 fresh garlic cloves
- 1–2 jalapeños (adjust to your heat preference)
- 400g (14oz) tin of chopped tomatoes
- Handful of fresh coriander
- Zest and juice of 1 lime
- Sea salt and freshly ground black pepper

There's nothing like the zing of a good salsa to wake up your taste buds and bring that backyard barbecue to life. This one's inspired by our time soaking up the sunshine (and street food) in Mexico, long before 'salsa' was something you just grabbed off a supermarket shelf. Whether it was served up with sizzling tacos or scooped with tortilla chips while watching the sunset, this punchy mix of tomatoes, jalapeño, lime and coriander became an instant favourite.

The magic of this salsa is in the balance – fresh, fiery, citrusy and herby all at once. It's a cinch to make, wildly customisable and honestly addictive. Try it with grilled chicken, use it to top a burger, spoon it over flame-cooked fish or keep it classic with a bowl of tortilla chips and some ice-cold drinks. Fresh, fast and packing serious flavour, this salsa might just steal the spotlight at your next barbecue.

Prep
Add the onion, garlic and jalapeños to a blender or food processor. Toss in the tomatoes, coriander, lime zest and juice, and season with salt and pepper. Pulse 2–5 times until you reach your desired salsa consistency. Don't over-blend, it should be chunky, not soupy.

Serve
Let it rest for 15 minutes before serving to let the flavours mingle and mellow. Store any leftovers in an airtight container in the fridge for 2–3 days.

LEMON & ROSEMARY MARINADE

A Mediterranean hug for chicken and pork

Prep Time: 5 minutes
Cook Time: 20 minutes

MAKES ABOUT 480ML (16FL OZ)

(ENOUGH FOR 4–6 PORTIONS OF MEAT)

60ml (2½fl oz) olive oil
2 garlic cloves, minced
Juice of 3 large lemons
1 heaped tbsp chopped fresh rosemary (or 2 tbsp dried)
2 tsp sea salt
½ tsp white pepper

If sunshine had a flavour, this would be it. Bright, citrusy and herb-packed, this marinade brings a beautiful Mediterranean vibe to your barbecue lineup. It's the kind of marinade that makes you want to crack open a crisp white wine, kick back in the garden and let the grill do its magic. It's a total game changer for chicken, pork chops or even skewers. It's clean, simple and bursting with flavour, and it works just as well for a quick midweek cook-up as it does for a weekend feast with friends.

Prep
Add the olive oil to a saucepan and gently fry the garlic for about 1 minute. Stir in the lemon juice, rosemary, salt and white pepper. Simmer over a low heat for 20 minutes to let the flavours infuse.

Serve
Allow to cool, then pour into an airtight container. Store in the fridge.

How to Use It
Pour over your meat and allow to marinate for at least an hour (longer for maximum flavour), then fire up the grill and enjoy the delicious citrus-herb char. Total barbecue bliss.

SMOKY GARLIC & CHILLI SAUCE

Mediterranean magic in a jar

Prep Time: 20 minutes
Cook Time: 20 minutes

MAKES ABOUT 480ML (16FL OZ)

2 tbsp extra virgin olive oil
1 large or 2 small onions, chopped
2 smoked garlic cloves (or 1 tsp if pre-minced)
1 red or green chilli, roughly chopped
2 tsp dried chilli flakes
400g (14oz) tin of chopped tomatoes
2 tbsp red pepper paste or tomato paste
1 tsp pomegranate molasses
1 tsp dried mint
Pinch each of salt and sugar
Small handful of fresh flat-leaf parsley, chopped

This bold, smoky garlic and chilli sauce is the ultimate Mediterranean flavour booster, perfect as a drizzle, dip or spread. It's rich with tomatoes, spiked with Turkish sweet red pepper paste and balanced with a sweet-sharp hit of pomegranate molasses. The smoked garlic gives it a deeper, more complex flavour that instantly elevates grilled meats, roasted veggies, flatbreads and more.

It's versatile and absolutely packed with flavour. Use it as a base for wraps, as a marinade, a sauce for grilled lamb, kebabs, falafel, grilled halloumi, or even breakfast eggs, or a punchy condiment on mezze platters. However you serve it, this smoky sauce brings serious Mediterranean soul to the plate. It keeps well, is easy to batch-make and adds a unique Mediterranean twist that guests will remember (and ask for again).

Prep

In a saucepan, heat the olive oil over a medium heat. Add the onions and sauté until soft and golden. Stir in the smoked garlic, chilli and chilli flakes and cook for 1–2 minutes until fragrant. Add the tomatoes, red pepper paste or tomato paste, pomegranate molasses, mint, salt and sugar. Simmer for 10–15 minutes until thickened slightly.

Remove from the heat. Add the chopped parsley and blend the sauce to your desired texture – smooth or slightly chunky.

Serve

Let cool before storing in jars. Keep in the fridge for up to a week or freeze in small portions for longer storage.

BACON ONION JAM
The ultimate burger upgrade

Prep Time: 10 minutes

Cook Time: 45–60 minutes

MAKES APPROX. 2 SMALL JARS

450g (1lb) streaky bacon, cut into 1cm (½in) strips

450g (1lb) yellow onions, thinly sliced

1 tbsp of your favourite BBQ rub or steak seasoning (I like something with heat here)

1 tbsp minced garlic

100g (3½oz) brown sugar

120ml (4fl oz) strong-brewed coffee

120ml (4fl oz) apple cider vinegar

120ml (4fl oz) maple syrup

¼ tsp dried thyme

If there's one thing I always want stacked on my burger (besides cheese, obviously), it's bacon onion jam. Inspired by a recipe from a buddy of mine, Chef Tom Jackson (ATBBQ – All Things Barbecue), I worked on this recipe for a Burger round at Qfest BBQ competition in 2018. I won the round with a first place, and I believe this recipe helped make that happen. It's been a go-to topping ever since. It's rich, sticky and ridiculously flavourful – the kind of jam that turns a good burger into a knockout. Spoon it over warm, add melty cheese and don't forget the napkins – it's messy, but that's the point.

This jam also works wonders with grilled sausages, flatbreads, served with a cheese board, a cheese on toast topper or even a spoon straight from the jar. This recipe makes enough for 6–8 burgers – or more if you're more restrained than I am!

Prep

Start by cooking the bacon in a cast-iron skillet over a medium heat until just golden and starting to crisp. Scoop it out with a slotted spoon and set it aside on a plate lined with kitchen paper. Leave a few tablespoons of the rendered fat in the pan.

Add the sliced onions to the pan with your seasoning blend. Stir regularly for 10–15 minutes until they become soft, golden and almost jammy. Stir in the garlic and brown sugar and cook for another minute until the sugar melts into the onions.

Pour in the coffee, cider vinegar and maple syrup. Stir well, scraping the bottom of the pan to lift any sticky bits. Add the thyme and return the bacon to the pan. Lower the heat and simmer, uncovered, for 25–30 minutes, or until the mixture is thick and glossy, stirring occasionally. If it looks dry before it's thick, add a splash of water.

Serve

Let it cool. For a finer texture, pulse the jam in a food processor until you reach your desired consistency. I like it chunky enough to spoon but smooth enough to spread.

Spoon into sterilised jars and keep it in the fridge for up to 2 weeks – if it lasts that long.

RUBS, SAUCES & CONDIMENTS

ROASTED GARLIC IN FOIL
Soft, sweet and BBQ-ready

Prep Time: 5 minutes

Cook Time: 30-40 minutes

MAKES 1 ROASTED GARLIC BULB
(ABOUT 1–2 TBSP SOFT GARLIC)

1 whole head of garlic
Olive oil, for drizzling
Salt (optional)

Roasting garlic on the barbecue brings out its rich, sweet, buttery character, no bitterness, just smooth flavour that melts into whatever it touches. Whether you're spreading it on bread, whisking it into dressings or stirring it through mash, this is one of those simple barbecue upgrades that makes everything taste better.

Prep
Slice about 5mm (¼in) off the top of the garlic head to expose the tops of the cloves. Place the garlic head on a square of foil. Drizzle generously with olive oil, letting it seep down into the cloves. Add a pinch of salt, if you like. Fold the foil into a tight pouch around the garlic to enclose it.

Set up your barbecue for indirect cooking at 180-200°C (350-400°F).

Grill
Place the foil packet on the cooler side of the grill, not directly over the flames. Close the lid and roast for 30-40 minutes, until the cloves are soft and lightly golden.

Serve
Let cool slightly, then squeeze the soft, roasted cloves from their skins like butter. Spread, mash or mix into anything that needs a hit of rich garlic flavour.

→ **Make a Compound Butter:** Mash into softened butter with herbs and a pinch of salt - perfect for steaks or corn.
→ **Upgrade Your Mash:** Stir through mashed potatoes or root veg for extra depth.
→ **Use in Sauces:** Add to mayo, aioli or salad dressings for a mellow garlic flavour.
→ **Spread It:** Serve with toasted bread for a simple snack or starter.
→ **Bulk Batch:** Roast several heads at once and store extras in olive oil in the fridge for a few days.

QUICK SPICY PICKLED RED ONIONS

Sharp, speedy and hot. A crunchy topper that cuts through rich meats and wakes up tacos, burgers and bowls

Prep Time:
10 minutes, plus 30 minutes pickling (better after 1-2 hours)

Cook Time:
5 minutes

SERVES 6–8

- 2 large red onions, thinly sliced
- 250ml (9fl oz) cider vinegar (or white wine vinegar)
- 125ml (4fl oz) hot water
- 1½ tbsp sugar
- 1 tsp sea salt
- 1 tsp dried chilli flakes (or 1 red chilli, thinly sliced)
- ½ tsp black peppercorns
- 1 garlic clove, sliced
- A few sprigs of fresh thyme (optional)

Meet the staple I want on every BBQ board: quick, spicy pickled red onions. They bring fast crunch, heat and tang that wakes up tacos, pulled pork, burgers... pretty much anything off the grill. Mix, pour and they're ready in minutes.

Prep
Pack the onions into a clean jar or heatproof container.

In a small saucepan, combine the vinegar, hot water, sugar, salt, chilli, peppercorns and garlic and thyme, if using. Bring just to a simmer, then remove from the heat. Pour the brine over the onions until fully submerged.

Serve
Let sit at room temperature for 30 minutes, or refrigerate for 1 hour before serving. Serve straight from the jar. Keep in the fridge for up to a week.

➔ **Add a BBQ Twist:** Add a splash of bourbon or smoked paprika to the brine before pouring.

APPLE SLAW
Crisp, sweet and built for the barbecue

Prep Time:
15 minutes, plus 15–30 minutes chilling (optional)

SERVES 6–8

- 300g (10oz) chopped cabbage (white or a mix)
- 1 red apple, unpeeled, cored and chopped
- 1 Granny Smith apple, unpeeled, cored and chopped
- 1 carrot, grated
- 90g (3½oz) red pepper, finely chopped
- 2 spring onions, finely chopped
- 75g (3oz) mayonnaise
- 70g (3oz) brown sugar
- 1 tbsp lemon juice

This crunchy apple slaw is the perfect sidekick for rich barbecue mains like ribs or pulled pork. The sweetness of red and green apples, the crunch of cabbage and carrot and the zing from lemon juice all come together in a creamy, tangy dressing that cuts through the smoke and fat like a dream. It's fresh, fast and made to be piled high in sandwiches or served on the side of a loaded barbecue plate.

Prep
In a large mixing bowl, combine the cabbage, both apples, grated carrot, red pepper and spring onions.

In a small bowl, whisk together the mayonnaise, brown sugar and lemon juice until smooth and well combined.

Pour the dressing over the slaw mixture and toss thoroughly until everything is evenly coated.

Serve
For best results, let the slaw chill in the fridge for 15–30 minutes before serving – but it's still brilliant straightaway.

→ **Add Heat:** Stir in a pinch of cayenne pepper or a chopped red chilli for a spicy kick.
→ **Swap the Mayo:** Use Greek yoghurt or a half-and-half mayo/yoghurt mix for a lighter version.
→ **Add Herbs:** A handful of chopped parsley or dill adds a fresh twist.
→ **Crunch Factor:** Toss in some toasted pecans, walnuts or pumpkin seeds for texture.
→ **Perfect Pairing:** Serve this with ribs, pulled pork sandwiches or BBQ chicken for a refreshing contrast.

COMPOUND BUTTERS
The BBQ secret weapon you didn't know you needed

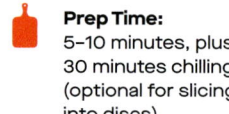

Prep Time:
5–10 minutes, plus 30 minutes chilling (optional for slicing into discs)

SERVES 4–6 PORTIONS

Here's the thing about barbecuing, sometimes it's the simplest things that make the biggest splash. Enter compound butters – those creamy, melty flavour bombs that can transform even the most humble cut of meat or charred veg into something straight-up irresistible.

We're talking easy mixes, big payoffs. Just swirl together a few key ingredients with good-quality butter and you've got yourself a barbecue sidekick that's as luxurious as it is effortless. Slather it over a resting steak, melt it onto grilled corn, or sneak a dollop into foil-roasted potatoes – watch the flavour level go from tasty to 'Where have you been all my life?'

These butters were born from playing around in the kitchen and trying to bottle some of our favourite flavours – from zesty lemon pepper to punchy Dijon and classic pesto. They're super handy to prep ahead, freeze beautifully, and will guarantee that your next grill-up ends on a high note.

PESTO BUTTER

Amazing on grilled chicken, lamb or even slathered on crusty bread.

90g (3½oz) butter, softened

Small bunch of fresh basil, finely chopped

2 tbsp grated Parmesan

Prep
Mix together the softened butter, chopped basil and Parmesan until smooth.

LEMON PEPPER BUTTER

Perfect for fish, prawns or charred asparagus.

90g (3½oz) butter, softened

1 tbsp lemon juice

2 tbsp lemon pepper seasoning

Prep
Mix together the butter, lemon juice and lemon pepper until smooth.

MUSTARD BUTTER

This one's a flavour-packed match for grilled sausages, pork chops or even a burger bun upgrade.

90g (3½oz) butter, softened

1 tbsp Dijon mustard

Prep
Mix together the butter and mustard until smooth.

CHILLI BUTTER

Slice and use as needed, or let it melt gloriously over hot-off-the-grill meats, veg or even stirred into rice or grilled corn.

115g (4oz) unsalted butter, softened

1 tsp garlic powder

1 tsp paprika

1 tsp chilli powder

½ tsp cayenne pepper

½ tsp kosher salt

⅛ tsp black pepper

Prep
Combine all the ingredients in a bowl and mix until fully incorporated.

Serve
Serve soft straight from the bowl, or roll into a log using cling film and refrigerate until firm and ready to slice.

COWBOY BUTTER
(Dippin' Gold)

Alright, this one isn't technically a compound butter, but we had to include it. Cowboy butter is served warm and melted, and it's absolutely perfect for dunking grilled meats, veg, crusty bread or seafood into.

115g (4oz) unsalted butter

Juice of ½ lemon

2 garlic cloves, finely grated

1 tsp Dijon or spicy brown mustard

½ tsp paprika

¼ tsp dried chilli flakes, or adjust to taste

Pinch each of salt and black pepper

Fresh parsley or chives (optional)

Prep
Melt the butter in a small saucepan or bowl. Stir in the lemon juice, garlic, mustard, paprika, chilli flakes, a pinch each of salt and pepper and fresh parsley or chives, if using.

Serve
Serve soft straight from the bowl, or roll into a log using cling film and refrigerate until firm and ready to slice.

Serve warm for dipping or drizzled over your barbecue spread.

CONVERSION TABLES

WEIGHTS

Metric	Imperial
15g	½ oz
25g	1 oz
40g	1½ oz
50g	2 oz
75g	3 oz
100g	4 oz
150g	5 oz
175g	6 oz
200g	7 oz
225g	8 oz
250g	9 oz
275g	10 oz
350g	12 oz
375g	13 oz
400g	14 oz
425g	15 oz
450g	1 lb
550g	1¼ lb
675g	1½ lb
900g	2 lb
1.5kg	3 lb
1.75kg	4 lb
2.25kg	5 lb

VOLUME

Metric	Imperial
25ml	1 fl oz
50ml	2 fl oz
85ml	3 fl oz
150ml	5 fl oz (¼ pint)
300ml	10 fl oz (½ pint)
450ml	15 fl oz (¾ pint)
600ml	1 pint
700ml	1¼ pints
900ml	1½ pints
1 litre	1¾ pints
1.2 litres	2 pints
1.25 litres	2¼ pints
1.5 litres	2½ pints
1.6 litres	2¾ pints
1.75 litres	3 pints
1.8 litres	3¼ pints
2 litres	3½ pints
2.1 litres	3¾ pints
2.25 litres	4 pints
2.75 litres	5 pints
3.4 litres	6 pints
3.9 litres	7 pints
5 litres	8 pints (1 gal)

MEASUREMENTS

Metric	Imperial
0.5cm	¼ inch
1cm	½ inch
2.5cm	1 inch
5cm	2 inches
7.5cm	3 inches
10cm	4 inches
15cm	6 inches
18cm	7 inches
20cm	8 inches
23cm	9 inches
25cm	10 inches
30cm	12 inches

OVEN TEMPERATURE

°C	FAN °C	°F	GAS MARK
140°C	120°C	275°F	Gas Mark 1
150°C	130°C	300°F	Gas Mark 2
160°C	140°C	325°F	Gas Mark 3
180°C	160°C	350°F	Gas Mark 4
190°C	170°C	375°F	Gas Mark 5
200°C	180°C	400°F	Gas Mark 6
220°C	200°C	425°F	Gas Mark 7
230°C	210°C	450°F	Gas Mark 8
240°C	220°C	475°F	Gas Mark 9

INDEX

apples
- 2-hour BBQ ribs with apple slaw & cider glaze 108
- apple slaw 245
- Irish-style porchetta with cider, apple & mustard crust 104

aubergines
- BBQ roasted vegetables 76

Aussie burger with the lot 204

avocados
- BBQ lobster tails with tropical salsa 122
- charred corn, avocado & smoked lime salad 54
- grilled elote street corn 72
- guacamole 230
- Mexico-inspired halloumi tacos 75
- zesty mango, halloumi & black bean salad 80

bacon
- the Aussie burger with the lot 204
- bacon onion jam 241
- bacon-wrapped onion rings 38
- BBQ cider caramelised onions 172
- BBQ shotgun shells 44
- Cheddar & bacon cornbread 58
- the Dubliner smash 204
- smash burgers 201
- smoky bacon, potato & corn chowder 92
- smoky jalapeño bacon poppers with BBQ cream cheese 48
- Texas-style beef chilli 180

BBQ sauce
- sticky pork belly burnt ends with sweet cider glaze 90
- sweet & smoky bourbon BBQ sauce 234

beans
- zesty mango, halloumi & black bean salad 80

béchamel sauce 186

beef
- BBQ shotgun shells 44
- beef roast with Cajun-spiced potato cakes 183
- brisket 32, 174–7, 196, 225–6
- cooking methods for steak 168
- crispy chilli beef 190–1
- flame-grilled burgers 170
- perfect sharing steak 168
- Philly cheese steak tear & share wheel 192
- pitmaster's pasta pie 184
- red wine braised short ribs 178
- rubs 224–9
- sesame-soy beef kebabs with homemade flatbreads 195
- smash burgers 201–4
- smoked beef brisket ragù 196
- smoky slow-cooked beef sharing platter 188
- surf & turf feast 118–121
- Texas-inspired smoked brisket 174–7
- Texas-style beef chilli 180
- Thor's hammer with creamy mash & hot honey veg 198

beer
- BBQ beer rolls 60
- Dubliner smash 204
- smoky slow-cooked beef sharing platter 188
- Thor's hammer with creamy mash & hot honey veg 198

berries
- peach & mascarpone French toast 219

bourbon BBQ sauce 234

bread
- BBQ beer rolls 60
- jalapeño cornbread 56–8
- peach & mascarpone French toast 219
- Philly cheese steak tear & share wheel 192
- sesame-soy beef kebabs with homemade flatbreads 195

brioche buns
- pulled pork with cider mop & tangy slaw 100
- smash burgers 201–4

briquettes 12–3, 25

brisket
- rubs 224–9
- slicing 32
- smoked beef brisket ragù 196
- Texas-inspired smoked brisket 174–7

Buffalo chicken potato skins 40

Buffalo hot wings 150

bulgur
- tabbouleh 59

burgers
- BBQ Portobello mushroom burgers with smoked Cheddar & chipotle mayo 83
- flame-grilled burgers 170
- smash burgers 201–5

butters
- roasted garlic in foil 242
- compound butters 246–7

cabbage
- 2-hour BBQ ribs with apple slaw & cider glaze 108
- apple slaw 245

Cajun-style fish with seared pineapple salsa 114

California-inspired fish tacos with avocado crema 126

campfire-style cooking 121, 178

carrots
- 2-hour BBQ ribs with apple slaw & cider glaze 108
- apple slaw 245
- Sunday roast BBQ lamb with roast veg & Yorkshire puds 136
- Thor's hammer with creamy mash & hot honey veg 198

carving meat 32

cast-iron cookware 9

cauliflower
- garam masala cauliflower steaks with mint chutney & pickled onions 86

cedar-planked teriyaki salmon 130

ceramic grills 16, 19, 22
- smoking wood on 29

charcoal chimneys 18

charcoal grills 14
- flame-grilled burgers 170
- smoking wood on 29

cheese
- BBQ Portobello mushroom burgers with smoked Cheddar & chipotle mayo 83
- BBQ roasted vegetables 76
- BBQ shotgun shells 44
- Buffalo chicken potato skins 40
- Cheddar & bacon cornbread 58
- cheese sauce 186
- cranberry & Parma ham tear & share with baked Camembert 43
- garlic butter & Parmesan-crusted hasselback potatoes 68
- grilled elote street corn 72
- mac & cheese with Tayto topping 53
- Mexico-inspired halloumi tacos 75
- Philly cheese steak tear & share wheel 192
- pitmaster's pasta pie 184
- smash burgers 201–5
- smoky jalapeño bacon poppers with BBQ cream cheese 48
- watermelon salad with feta & olives 46
- zesty mango, halloumi & black bean salad 80

chicken
    BBQ chicken shawarma 146
    Buffalo chicken potato skins 40
    Buffalo hot wings 150
    dynamite popcorn chicken with pickled cucumber & flatbreads 154
    spatchcock chicken with garlic herb butter 164
    spiced chicken skewers with lemon-mint yoghurt 158
    sriracha & lime grilled chicken wings 160
    sticky peanut chicken skewers 152
chilli butter 247
chimichurri 183, 204, 235
chipotle beef rub, all-purpose 227
chocolate
    BBQ chocolate muffins in orange skins 208
    skillet cookie dough 216
    Texas-style beef chilli 180
cider
    BBQ cider caramelised onions 172
    Irish cider apple & honey BBQ sauce 38, 90, 231
    Irish-style porchetta with cider, apple & mustard crust 104
    pulled pork with cider mop & tangy slaw 100
    sticky pork belly burnt ends with sweet cider glaze 90
citrus herb seafood rub 229
cleaning the barbecue 8
coconut
    boozy grilled rum-infused pineapple 213
coconut milk
    Gold Coast-inspired coconut & lime shrimp skewers 128
coffee
    bacon onion jam 241
    Texas-style beef chilli 180
cola-glazed ham with black pepper & marmalade glaze & proper Yorkshire puds 96–7
corn
    charred corn, avocado & smoked lime salad 54
    grilled elote street corn 72
    Mexico-inspired halloumi tacos 75
    smoky bacon, potato & corn chowder 92
cornbread
    jalapeño cornbread 56–8
cowboy butter 247
cranberry & Parma ham tear & share with baked Camembert 43
cream cheese
    key lime pie 214
    smoky jalapeño bacon poppers with BBQ cream cheese 48
crisps
    mac & cheese with Tayto topping 53
crispy chilli beef 190–1
cucumber
    BBQ lobster tails with tropical salsa 122
    crisp cucumber & fennel salad 50
    dynamite popcorn chicken with pickled cucumber & flatbreads 154
    KG Egyptian-inspired salad 64
    tabbouleh 59
curry yoghurt lamb cutlets 138

direct and indirect zones 20
Dubliner smash 205
dynamite popcorn chicken with pickled cucumber & flatbreads 154

electric lighters 18
equipment 8, 9

fennel
crisp cucumber & fennel salad 50
feta
    grilled elote street corn 72
    watermelon salad with feta & olives 46
    zesty mango, halloumi & black bean salad 80
fire lighting & management 16–19
fire triangle 24–5
firelighters 18
fish
    Cajun-style fish with seared pineapple salsa 114
    California-inspired fish tacos with avocado crema 126
    citrus herb seafood rub 229
flatbreads 157, 194
    BBQ chicken shawarma 146
    dynamite popcorn chicken with pickled cucumber & flatbreads 154
    herby lemon lamb kebabs with warm flatbreads & fiery garlic sauce 142
fuel 8, 12–14

garam masala cauliflower steaks with mint chutney & pickled onions 86
garlic
    garlic butter 242
    garlic butter & Parmesan-crusted hasselback potatoes 68
    heirloom tomato & roasted garlic galette 78
    herby lemon lamb kebabs with warm flatbreads & fiery garlic sauce 142
    red wine braised short ribs 178
    roasted garlic in foil 242
    smoky garlic & chilli sauce 240
    spatchcock chicken with garlic herb butter 164
gas grills
    creating zones 22
    flame-grilled burgers 170
    lighting 16
    smoking wood on 29
gas lighters 18
Gold Coast-inspired coconut & lime shrimp skewers 128
guacamole 230
Guinness 198, 204

halloumi
    Mexico-inspired halloumi tacos 75
    zesty mango, halloumi & black bean salad 80
ham
    cola-glazed ham with black pepper & marmalade glaze & proper Yorkshire puds 96–7
    cranberry & Parma ham tear & share with baked Camembert 43
    heirloom tomato & roasted garlic galette 78
herby lemon lamb kebabs with warm flatbreads & fiery garlic sauce 142
honey
    Buffalo hot wings 150
    Irish cider apple & honey BBQ sauce 38, 90, 231
    pineapple & chilli salsa 236
    smoky grilled peaches with Cointreau & rosemary 210
    sriracha & lime grilled chicken wings 160
    sticky pork belly burnt ends with sweet cider glaze 90
    sweet & smoky bourbon BBQ sauce 234
    Thor's hammer with creamy mash & hot honey veg 198
hot air lighters 18

Irish cider apple & honey BBQ sauce 38, 90, 231
Irish-style porchetta with cider, apple & mustard crust 104

jalapeños
    Cajun-style fish with seared pineapple salsa 114
    California-inspired fish tacos with avocado crema 126
    fiery fresh salsa 238
    jalapeño cornbread 56–8
    pineapple & chilli salsa 236

smoky jalapeño bacon poppers with BBQ cream cheese 48
spicy pork chops with mango salsa 95
jamón Ibérico
  heirloom tomato & roasted garlic galette 78

kamado-style grills 19, 29, 178
kettle grills 16, 22
key lime pie 214

lamb
  chilli lamb skewers with ginger & soy slaw 141
  curry yoghurt lamb cutlets 138
  herby lemon lamb kebabs with warm flatbreads & fiery garlic sauce 142
  mint & parsley sauce for smoked lamb racks 235
  sticky apricot & mustard-glazed lamb chops 134
  Sunday roast BBQ lamb with roast veg & Yorkshire puds 136
layering rubs 31
leeks
  BBQ-seared leek barrels with smoky romesco sauce 84
lemons
  BBQ chicken shawarma 146
  citrus herb seafood rub 229
  herby lemon lamb kebabs with warm flatbreads & fiery garlic sauce 142
  lemon & rosemary marinade 239
  lemon pepper butter 247
  spatchcock chicken with garlic herb butter 164
  spiced chicken skewers with lemon-mint yoghurt 158
  tabbouleh 59
limes
  2-hour BBQ ribs with apple slaw & cider glaze 108
  BBQ lobster tails with tropical salsa 122
  BBQ shrimp with mango lime vinaigrette 116
  Cajun-style fish with seared pineapple salsa 114
  California-inspired fish tacos with avocado crema 126
  charred corn, avocado & smoked lime salad 54
  fiery fresh salsa 238
  garam masala cauliflower steaks with mint chutney & pickled onions 86
  Gold Coast-inspired coconut & lime shrimp skewers 128
  grilled elote street corn 72
  guacamole 230
  key lime pie 214
  peach cobbler in tin coffee cups 220
  pineapple & chilli salsa 236
  smoky slow-cooked beef sharing platter 188
  soy-glazed scallops with ginger & spring onion 112
  spicy pork chops with mango salsa 95
  sriracha & lime grilled chicken wings 160
lobster
  BBQ lobster tails with tropical salsa 122
lumpwood charcoal 12, 19, 25

mac & cheese with Tayto topping 53
mangoes
  BBQ lobster tails with tropical salsa 122
  BBQ shrimp with mango lime vinaigrette 116
  spicy pork chops with mango salsa 95
  zesty mango, halloumi & black bean salad 80
  maple & mustard pork rub 228
marmalade
  cola-glazed ham with black pepper & marmalade glaze & proper Yorkshire puds 96–7
masala smash 205
meat
  resting 32
  slicing or carving 32
Mexico-inspired halloumi tacos 75
mint

curry yoghurt lamb cutlets 138
garam masala cauliflower steaks with mint chutney & pickled onions 86
mint & parsley sauce for smoked lamb racks 235
mojo-style pork roast 102
spiced chicken skewers with lemon-mint yoghurt 158
tabbouleh 59
mojo-style pork roast 102
mushrooms
  BBQ Portobello mushroom burgers with smoked Cheddar & chipotle mayo 83
mussels
  surf & turf feast 118–121
mustard
  Irish-style porchetta with cider, apple & mustard crust 104
  mustard butter 247
  sticky apricot & mustard-glazed lamb chops 134

Oklahoma onion smash 202
olives
  watermelon salad with feta & olives 46
onions
  bacon onion jam 241
  bacon-wrapped onion rings 38
  BBQ cider caramelised onions 172
  Dubliner smash 205
  garam masala cauliflower steaks with mint chutney & pickled onions 86
  Oklahoma onion smash 202
  Portobello mushroom burgers with smoked Cheddar & chipotle mayo 83
oranges
  BBQ chocolate muffins in orange skins 208
  cola-glazed ham with black pepper & marmalade glaze & proper Yorkshire puds 96–7
  mojo-style pork roast 102
  peach cobbler in tin coffee cups 220

parsnips
  Sunday roast BBQ lamb with roast veg & Yorkshire puds 136
pasta
  BBQ shotgun shells 44
  mac & cheese with Tayto topping 53
  smoked beef brisket ragù 196
peaches
  peach & mascarpone French toast 218
  peach cobbler in tin coffee cups 220
  smoky grilled peaches with Cointreau & rosemary 210
peanut butter
  skillet cookie dough 216
  sticky peanut chicken skewers 152
pellet smokers 29
peppers
  2-hour BBQ ribs with apple slaw & cider glaze 108
  apple slaw 245
  BBQ roasted vegetables 76
  BBQ-seared leek barrels with smoky romesco sauce 84
  charred corn, avocado & smoked lime salad 54
  chimichurri smash 205
  chunky tomato relish 237
  crispy chilli beef 190–1
  fire-roasted tomato & pepper relish 173
  mac & cheese with Tayto topping 53
  pineapple & chilli salsa 236
  spiced chicken skewers with lemon-mint yoghurt 158
  Texas-style beef chilli 180
pesto butter 247
Philly cheese steak tear & share wheel 192
pineapple
  Aussie burger with the lot 204

boozy grilled rum-infused pineapple 213
Cajun-style fish with seared pineapple salsa 114
pineapple & chilli salsa 236
pitmaster's pasta pie 184
pork
  2-hour BBQ ribs with apple slaw & cider glaze 108
  Irish-style porchetta with cider, apple & mustard crust 104
  maple & mustard pork rub 228
  mojo-style pork roast 102
  pulled pork with cider mop & tangy slaw 100
  smokehouse stack 204
  spicy pork chops with mango salsa 95
  sticky pork belly burnt ends with sweet cider glaze 90
Portobello mushroom burgers with smoked Cheddar & chipotle mayo 83
potatoes
  BBQ crispy potato salad with mustard-caper dressing 62
  BBQ roasted vegetables 76
  beef roast with Cajun-spiced potato cakes 183
  Buffalo chicken potato skins 40
  garlic butter & Parmesan-crusted hasselback potatoes 68
  salt & chilli BBQ wedges 70
  smoky bacon, potato & corn chowder 92
  Thor's hammer with creamy mash & hot honey veg 198
prawns
  BBQ shrimp with mango lime vinaigrette 116
  citrus herb seafood rub 229
  Gold Coast-inspired coconut & lime shrimp skewers 128
  surf & turf feast 118–121
preheating the grill 8
puff pastry
  cranberry & Parma ham tear & share with baked Camembert 43
  heirloom tomato & roasted garlic galette 78

ragù
  pitmaster's pasta pie 184
  smoked beef brisket ragù 196
red onions
  BBQ roasted vegetables 76
  Cajun-style fish with seared pineapple salsa 114
  fire-roasted tomato & pepper relish 173
  quick spicy pickled red onions 244
  spiced chicken skewers with lemon-mint yoghurt 158
  Sunday roast BBQ lamb with roast veg & Yorkshire puds 136
red wine braised short ribs 178
resting meat 32
roasting, temperatures for 10
rosemary
  lemon & rosemary marinade 239
  smoky grilled peaches with Cointreau & rosemary 210
rubs 31, 174, 224–9
rum
  boozy grilled rum-infused pineapple 213

salads
  BBQ crispy potato salad with mustard caper dressing 62
  crisp cucumber & fennel salad 50
  KG Egyptian-inspired salad 64
  tabbouleh 59
  watermelon salad with feta & olives 46
salmon
  cedar-planked teriyaki salmon 130
salsas 95, 114, 122, 236, 238
scallops
  citrus herb seafood rub 229
  soy-glazed scallops with ginger & spring onion 112–13
seasoning 8, 26–7
sesame-soy beef kebabs with homemade flatbreads 194

shallots
  red wine braised short ribs 178
skillet cookie dough 216
slaws 100, 108, 140, 245
smash burgers 201–5
smoked beef brisket ragù 196
smokehouse stack 204
smoking
  chicken 164
  clean vs dirty smoke 29
  smoky slow-cooked beef sharing platter 188
  surf & turf feast 121
  temperatures for 10
  Texas-inspired smoked brisket 174–7
  wood 28–9
soy-glazed scallops with ginger & spring onion 112–13
spatchcock chicken with garlic herb butter 164
spring onions
  2-hour BBQ ribs with apple slaw & cider glaze 108
  apple slaw 245
  BBQ crispy potato salad with mustard caper dressing 62
  crispy chilli beef 190–1
  salt & chilli BBQ wedges 70
  soy-glazed scallops with ginger & spring onion 112–13
  sticky peanut chicken skewers 152
sriracha & lime grilled chicken wings 160
sugar snap peas
  2-hour BBQ ribs with apple slaw & cider glaze 108
Sunday roast BBQ lamb with roast veg & Yorkshire puds 136
surf & turf feast 118–121
sweet potatoes 183

tabbouleh 59, 142
tacos 75, 115, 126
temperatures 10
teriyaki sauce
  cedar-planked teriyaki salmon 130
  smash 202
Tex-Mex smash 205
Texas-style beef chilli 180
thermometers 9, 10
Thor's hammer with creamy mash & hot honey veg 198
tomatoes
  BBQ roasted vegetables 76
  charred corn, avocado & smoked lime salad 54
  chunky tomato relish 237
  fiery fresh salsa 238
  fire-roasted tomato & pepper relish 173
  guacamole 230
  heirloom tomato & roasted garlic galette 78
  KG Egyptian-inspired salad 64
  smoky garlic & chilli sauce 240
  tabbouleh 59

watermelon salad with feta & olives 46
wok cooking 191
wood
  combining charcoal and wood 14
  hardwood chunks 25
  kindling 18
  smoking wood 28–9

yoghurt
  curry yoghurt lamb cutlets 138
  garam masala cauliflower steaks with mint chutney & pickled onions 86
  spiced chicken skewers with lemon-mint yoghurt 158
Yorkshire puds 96–7

zones for cooking 20–3

THANKS

First and foremost, a huge thank you to everyone who's followed, supported, and shared along the way. Without you, this book simply wouldn't exist.

To my wife Rom, who's involved in all the madness at every step, from the first spark of a recipe idea to helping capture the content, thank you for your patience, support and good humour. To Caidan and Orin and my wider family, my chief food tasters, supporters and my most honest critics, thanks for every 'one more bite' and late-night sample.

To the friends who helped me get here, most notably Elky, Ben and Conor, your encouragement, support and friendship has meant everything. Mick, no longer with us but very much present in the memories, laughs and stories woven through this book and recipes.

Huge thanks to my publishing team Oscar, Sam and Rosie for steering me through this process and helping deliver my first book. Your calm guidance has turned my scribbles and ideas into pages that I'm proud of.

Valerie, Charlie, Max and Liz, for your talent and vision bringing my recipes to life, capturing the colour, the flames and the spirit of what BBQ's all about.

It would also be remiss of me not to mention my old crew for the laughs, support and steady encouragement.

Onlyslaggin is an ode to Irish friendships and humour; I hope that spirit comes through on every page.

EBURY PRESS

UK | USA | Canada | Ireland | Australia
India | New Zealand | South Africa

Ebury Press is part of the Penguin Random House group of companies whose addresses
can be found at global.penguinrandomhouse.com

Penguin Random House UK
One Embassy Gardens, 8 Viaduct Gardens, London SW11 7BW

penguin.co.uk
global.penguinrandomhouse.com

First published by Ebury Press in 2026

1

Copyright © Jim Moore 2026
Photography © Liz and Max Haarala Hamilton 2026

The moral right of the author has been asserted.

No part of this book may be used or reproduced in any manner for the purpose of training artificial intelligence technologies or systems. In accordance with Article 4(3) of the DSM Directive 2019/790, Penguin Random House expressly reserves this work from the text and data mining exception.

Editorial Director: Sam Crisp
Senior Editor: Rosie Pearce
Senior Production Manager: Lucy Harrison
Designer: Studio Nic+Lou
Illustration: Harriet Smeaton
Photographers: Liz and Max Haarala Hamilton
Food Stylist: Valerie Berry
Prop Stylist: Charlie Phillips

Colour origination by Altaimage Ltd
Printed and bound in Germany by MOHN Media

The authorised representative in the EEA is Penguin Random House Ireland,
Morison Chambers, 32 Nassau Street, Dublin D02 YH68.

A CIP catalogue record for this book is available from the British Library

ISBN 9781529975758

Penguin Random House is committed to a sustainable future for our business,
our readers and our planet. This book is made from Forest Stewardship Council® certified paper.